Johnnie the One

The John Charles Story

Johnnie the One

The John Charles Story

Brian Belton

TEMPUS

This book is dedicated to John and Clive Charles,
Canning Town boys who made football history

A proportion of the proceeds from the sale of this book will be
donated to the St Francis Hospice at Havering-atte-Bower,
which cared for John Charles in his final days

First published 2004

Tempus Publishing Ltd
The Mill, Brimscombe Port
Stroud, Gloucestershire GL5 2QG
www.tempus-publishing.com

British Library Cataloguing in Publication Data.
A catalogue record for this book is available from the British Library.

ISBN 0 7524 2570 6

Typesetting and origination by Tempus Publishing.
Printed and bound in Great Britain.

Contents

'Charlo', the first black Hammer.

The Player's Foreword

'Indecision is one way of playing right into the opposition's hands. Move confidently and decisively at every opportunity.'

(*The Strategy of Soccer* – Johnny Byrne)

What follows is the first part of the address given by Brian Dear at the funeral service of John Charles on 30 August 2002. It is included with the permission of John's wife Carol, and Brian, a former Upton Park favourite (the first of only two post-war Hammers and one of the very few footballers to score 5 goals in a single game played at the highest level). Brian first got to know John when they were kids playing against each other in schoolboy football, with John for West Ham and Brian for East Ham. They bridged the East/West divide and joined forces as youngsters and mature professionals, fighting West Ham United's cause for well over a decade. After football they remained extremely close friends. Brian was at John's bedside when he passed away peacefully at 10.45 p.m. at home in Barkingside on the night of Saturday 17 August 2002.

John the footballer

One of my first memories of John was from Ernie Gregory, West Ham's former long-serving goalkeeper, who was sent by the manager, Ted Fenton, to watch a West Ham schoolboy game at the Spotted Dog Ground. Ernie's instructions were to look at a lad called Peter Turner, who eventually, after playing for England Schoolboys, joined Arsenal. Ernie returned to Upton Park and gave Ted the now well-known message: 'Turner looked a good player but it was the little black kid at centre half who caught my eye.' So the legend began.

John William Charles

John joined the West Ham Ground staff in the 1960/61 season. It was not long before J.W. Charles was shortened to 'Charlo', which until this day had been his name to all who met him and enjoyed his friendship.

Charlo was the captain and centre half of a very elite youth side which won the FA Youth Cup in 1963. The team – Mackleworth, Burnett, Kitchener, Dawkins, Charlo, Howe, Redknapp, Bennett, Britt, Sissons and Dryden, triumphed over the two-legged

The West Ham goalkeeper, Ernie Gregory, punches clear from a Birmingham City attack during the Second Division match at Upton Park. Frank O'Farrell, the Hammer's left-half, is to the left. Birmingham's Kinsey challenges Gregory. The Blues won 1-2, with Birmingham scoring all three goals (the Midlanders' number five, Newman, put through his own net).

final against Liverpool, with Tommy Smith included. They won 5-2 on aggregate after being 1-3 down from the first leg. What a result!

It goes without saying that most of those lads made first-team appearances later in their careers. Charlo went on to win England Youth caps on five occasions, as did other members of that winning team of 1963.

Charlo the player

Charlo soon became one of 'Ernie's boys'. Being one of Ernie's boys enabled you to be given a baptism of fire in the Metropolitan League or the 'A' Team. Nobody escaped. Hurst, Peters, Bickles, Boyce, Burkett, Bovington, plus myself and many others served the cause. At Didcot, Bedford, Haywards Heath, Tonbridge, Eastbourne and against the Metropolitan Police, no prisoners were taken in those days and in those games.

Charlo was now becoming a cultured, no-nonsense left-back, and remained so for the rest of his career. The next step was the Reserves, which of course were much more civilised. They had better pitches plus hotel food, which was a far cry from the 5 bob tea-money spent at the roadside café on the way to Didcot!

Charlo's first taste of the big time came in May 1963 against Blackburn Rovers in Division One of the Football League at Upton Park. West Ham were beaten by the only goal of the game. Just for the record, in his debut game, Charlo wore the number 6 shirt of West Ham's favourite son, Bobby Moore. Respect to Bobby, who wore number 5 that day. Bobby quickly got his number 6 shirt back – respect for Charlo.

First team squad, 1961/62.

Two years went by before Charlo gained a regular place in the first team and the time finally arrived for him to play in some of the memorable games of the mid-sixties. One such match was against Manchester United. It was the last home game of the season and it drew the biggest crowd seen at Upton Park since the Second World War. United beat the Hammers 1-6 to clinch the Division One title. Not only did Charlo have Best, Charlton, Law and Kidd to deal with, he scored West Ham's only goal and, some pundits say, the best of the seven scored that day. More respect goes to Charlo.

(Here Brian broke off for a second and his voice quavered just a little.)

Me hands are trembling and I ain't had a drink for eight years!

(The congregation laughed softly as a gentle empathy undulated through the crowded little chapel. Taking strength, as only a five-goals-in-one-game scorer can, and a deep breath, Brian resumed.)

Charlo later suffered a spate of injuries and was forced to miss many games. He left West Ham in 1971, having played close to 150 League and Cup games. Charlo never played for another club.

Charlo was a great teammate who always gave one hundred per cent. Football is surely indebted to him as he undoubtedly paved the way for his black brothers who now enjoy the fame, riches and adulation which he most certainly helped make possible. He was a true Hammer.

Brian Dear

'Never get despondent if you find yourself 'bottom of the class'. Hearten yourself with the knowledge that you can improve. With such thoughts in mind you might well be quite capable of surprising yourself with your eventual progress.'

(*The Strategy of Soccer* – Johnny Byrne)

The Supporter's Foreword

'The body has an important part to play. It should be between the ball and a rival and it should help maintain your balance.'

(The Strategy of Soccer – Johnny Byrne)

This book is a memorial but also a celebration of the life of John Charles, not the legendary 'gentle giant' of Leeds United, Juventus and Wales fame, but the 'Charlo' (as fellow players and fans knew him) of Canning Town, West Ham and England Youth – the first black player to represent the club at first-team level.

John never won full international honours like some of his more famous contemporaries. He was not to be in any XI that won major trophies. However, he more than held his own in Division One of the Football League. Throughout his entire career he played at the highest level of the English game. John took the field alongside Peters, Hurst, Moore and Greaves. He of course played against the great Jimmy and also faced the likes of Law, Charlton and George Best, all of whom would walk into any Premiership team of today.

He was an honest dependable full-back who got on with the game without complaint and his style of play could perhaps be best described as uncompromising. Other adjectives that would equally apply are hard-tackling, tough, tenacious and above all resilient. However, it would be wrong to think that he was not skilful, as he certainly was, and he was also a locally born Hammer who played for no other club, which is something that is becoming increasingly rare with the influx of foreign players. I watched him play from his earliest days at the club and later got to know him as a person. He was West Ham through and through.

Terry Connelly

'Quickness of recovery is another vital asset. The best defender is the one who, once beaten, can turn smartly and get in another tackle. Try quick turning, first one way and then the other.'

(The Strategy of Soccer – Johnny Byrne)

Introduction

'Never be afraid or unco-operative if asked to fill a gap in another position.'
(The Strategy of Soccer – Johnny Byrne)

This book is the story of one man, John William Charles; 'Charlo' as his fellow players, friends and the Upton Park supporters christened him from his earliest days in football, or, as he occasionally called himself, 'Johnnie the One'. His life and career in football were bound up with what was to be the pinnacle of achievement for West Ham United Football Club. This period encompassed the side's first FA Cup win, their first and last success on the European stage, the Inter-Toto ('Inter-Two-bob', 'Into-Lego') Cup notwithstanding, and, under the leadership of West Ham's young skipper Bobby Moore and with goals from two of the rising stars of the East End, Martin Peters and Geoff Hurst, England's victory in the 1966 World Cup. As such, John's young life was entwined with the history of his club. However, the following pages, which were written over the last five years of John's life, will concentrate on this extraordinary, ordinary man as part of and a contributor to the development of West Ham United, but also as a unique person.

John was born in Canning Town, East London on 20 September 1944. He was to become a pioneer of sport, albeit unwittingly. He was the first black player to break into West Ham's first team, one of the first to play at the top level of the modern English game and the first black player to represent England when he gained the first of his Youth caps. That is a lot of 'firsts'. As such he led the way for other black professionals to compete for selection at West Ham and the highest echelon of English, British and European football. John created this path during the early 1960s, which were the most difficult years in terms of football's and Britain's transition to multiculturalism. He was glad to tell me about this time and although I think he was surprised by my interest, John willingly gave me his own words, and I have used them faithfully, alongside those of his most immediate family and some of his closest friends.

All of us, the writer and those who helped with the writing, share a similar background and accent. We use the same colloquialisms and metaphors. There are shared values and humour. As such, as far as possible I have attempted to preserve the shape and form of this language. I have tried, where possible, to hold onto the words, inflection and grammar of the East London community, out of which John, his family and myself grew. After all, this was the means John used to express himself and part of the foundation on which he built his footballing vocabulary. To those who would complain

Half the Preston team look on as the eighteen-year-old John Sissons levels the score, becoming the youngest player to score in a Wembley Final.

that this is not perfect English I would agree, but answer that the syntax used is as close as I can get to 'good Canning Town', the identity that John Charles was most proud of. The book is about him and not some idea of perfect grammar (as if such a thing existed). We are, in many ways, shaped by our language. The way John played and spoke perhaps best expressed the person he was: strong, loyal, protective and joyful.

In the effort to tell the story of John Charles, one cannot help but include a particular view of West Ham United in the sixties. The club, of course, is part of football in general. This being the case, the pages that follow reflect on the immense changes in the game that have occurred in John's all too short lifetime. Not least of these has been the significance of the broad entry of black players into the English game and their contribution towards its growth and development. It is also impossible to write about John without some consideration of the area he was born into. It is a district that has a symbiotic relationship with West Ham United. It has helped to define what the club is. The identity of the communities that make up the London Borough of Newham, the 'localities' that nestle around the Boleyn Ground, West and East Ham, Upton Park, Plaistow, Canning Town, Manor Park, Forest Gate, Silver Town and Custom House, are associated and bound up with the club. All 'are' West Ham.

This being the case, as you read you might begin to understand how the East End evolved from wartime devastation to the romantic badlands of swinging-sixties London. John's life will take you through the slump and economic transition of the seventies and eighties that took a toll on the Charles family. Finally, this family will talk to you in the context of the twenty-first century, which offers a very different view of the world to John's grandchildren compared to the perspective he had from the vantage point of Ordinance Road E16 back in the late 1940s.

So, what you are about to embark on is essentially the narrative of one man's journey, but it is, at the same time, the tale of a family built by a family. It is also a story about a football club – West Ham United. The Hammers' progress in the FA Youth Cup, the trophy through which John began to establish himself at Upton Park, is woven into this history. What follows is about a game, a community, a society and a time. And, as all things melt into one, all this meets in *Johnnie the One*.

'Generally speaking, passing is a two-man movement and the receiver has just as important a part to play as the man who is attempting to put him in possession.'
(*The Strategy of Soccer* – Johnny Byrne)

Throughout this book I have included quotes from The Strategy of Soccer *by Johnny Byrne. Budgie, as he was known to fans and players alike, was a close friend of John Charles. He died just a few years before John and, like him, was lost to football and the world long before natural justice might allow. As such, his words and philosophy will act to remind us that football is a closed discipline, but, like everything else, can be linked to the rest of the world by the actions of our minds. If you look closely, Budgie, like Johnnie, has much help and knowledge to give.*

1

Writing Football,
Writing about John Charles

'Moderation in everything should be the rule'.

(*The Strategy of Soccer* – Johnny Byrne)

I have written a number of books which focus on the history of West Ham United. In particular I have concentrated on this club's most creative and productive years that spanned the two decades between 1950 and 1970. In the process of this work, I have had to wade through part of the ocean of literary detritus that football has produced. This has caused me, in the writing of this book, to steer away from the usual football biography format, which turns players (human beings) into one of three species of cheap crypto-fictional caricature – a kind of pallid saint, a 'shock, horror, probe' monster (a lurid tabloid villain) or a stereotypical, seaside postcard/*Carry On* movie 'bloke'. Whatever the pastiche, the portrayal is usually overlaid with what the great American sports writer, Red Smith, called the 'gee-whiz' school of sports writing, a sycophancy that produces a narrative which has little resemblance to a lived life. In short, it is a kind of parody, which, as John might have said, 'takes the piss'. This kind of burlesque has helped to eat the heart out of football in Britain over the years. It can be summed up by the picture of the legendary footballing Falstaff figure, Neil Ruddock, on the cover of his autobiography, *Hell Razor* (1999). It is a 'close-up' of him with two fingers stuck up his nostrils, in 'flicking the V's' mode. *Hell Razor* is a laddish dirge and typical of the blandness of spirit that is assaulting the morale of the long-suffering supporter of football. At the time of the publication of his autobiography, the rotund Razor was still making up the numbers at Upton Park, and many loyal Hammers fans bought the book only because of that fact. Within a few weeks he had moved on to Crystal Palace on, as it turned out, an equally temporary basis.

I have also attempted to avoid peppering the following pages with references to or quotes from other players, managers or coaches, as this would risk obliterating the person who was John Charles, the subject and the reason for the book's existence. I have tried to demonstrate his development and something of what arose from his presence at Upton Park – his contribution to the progress of West Ham United. This being the case, I have included descriptions of some of the most memorable and important matches John was involved in, but not the ones that are always covered in histories of the Hammers. There are victories and defeats. That is the reality of football, especially West Ham's football. I have tried, as much as possible, to only write about matches I attended that were truly seminal games for John. This is why I have traced the development of West Ham in the FA Youth Cup, a tradition taken up by Charlo and the lads he skippered in the Hammers' 1963 triumph. It is why I detail a match against Real Madrid played in the Astrodome, Texas, a second-round European Cup Winners Cup clash in Greece, West Ham's confrontation with an Egyptian national XI in Cairo, as well as League games that John saw as milestones in his career.

I hope that *Johnnie the One* will not just be received as just another 'football book' but also as a work that will add to the continuing history of the contribution of black people to sport and wider society, which is part of our shared social history.

'Positional play even without the ball is most important. The thinking player will see a move building up and, on occasions, he will find that by moving around he can divert attention from the main build-up of the attack.'

(The Strategy of Soccer – Johnny Byrne)

2

From the Heartland

'As you move up to an opponent you will find it a help to accentuate your "lean" and then move the other way.'

(*The Strategy of Soccer* – Johnny Byrne)

Less than two weeks before John Charles first saw light, Italy had unconditionally surrendered to the Allies following the invasion of the Italian mainland by British and Canadian troops across the straits of Messina from Sicily. Just four days before John was born, West Ham United had beaten Queens Park Rangers at Loftus Road in the Wartime League South. The Hammers' immortal Len Goulden had scored the only goal of the game. This was the first of nine consecutive away games. West Ham won them all, including a 3-0 victory over Arsenal in front of a crowd of 27,800. The Hammers had not played before that many spectators since they had beaten Blackburn Rovers in the Football League War Cup Final in 1940. The team that defeated the Gunners so thoroughly were: Harry Medhurst, Jones, Harry Lewis, Burnett, Ted Fenton, Norman Corbett, Terry Woodgate, Richard Dunn, Dodds, Goulden and Jackie Wood. Goulden and Dodds got a goal each before an Arsenal own-goal finished the game.

John was born into a big family. He told me:

I was number eight of nine children, all different colours. [John smiled.] *There was Jessie, Josie, Bon, Len, Bonzo, Marge and Rita. Clive came later. One died. I just keep mainly in contact with me sister Rita and Clive and Bon and Marge. My dad, who originally came to Britain from Grenada in the West Indies, was a seaman. They called him 'Gentleman Charles'. Mum was always a housewife. The four eldest were white (there were five, Michael got killed) then there was Bonzo and Margie, they were sort of tan. Their dad was black but they didn't come out that way.* [He chortled.] *They were olive colour, yeah. And then my dad was black but we come out black.* [John then smiled the smile I came to know so well over the near half a decade I spent researching this book. It was an expression of a man who could give a look that asked if you were comfortable and at the same time told you that he was comfortable.] *My sister, Rita, she was older than me (still is).* [He smiled again]. *And then, seven years after me, there was Clive. So I was second from youngest, but the youngest up till I was seven. I was me dad's first son, so I was looked after and made a bit*

John Charles on Gooner turf.

of a fuss of. Mum kept us pretty clean for a big family. Me and me sister were
close, we still are. She's always round, 'How are yer?' and that.

However, because of his place of birth, John was part of a much wider set of relations:
'I was born in Canning Town, Ordinance Road, right bang opposite Rathbone Street.'

This was the heartland of support for West Ham United, where the East End's football
club had been born. John told of some of the difficulties associated with a mixed-race
marriage at the time:

My mum was from Silver Town. The old man was in digs down that way and
that's how they met. My mum was white. She got called everything, from
whatever to whatever. Even her family walked on the other side of the street,
except for old uncle Owen, me mum's brother, he was alright. He was at our
wedding. All the others was dead I think. [John laughed.]

My mum was great, she was brilliant. She had three husbands! She died in
May 1994. She was about eighty-five. She was as tough as nails! She was as
tough as boots that little old lady. Her name was Jessie. My dad was her third
husband. He was the best one. [John laughed quietly.] *His name was Moister*
Leopold. I never saw me grandparents. Never been to Grenada, might go one
day. I might have a plot of land out there. [John chuckled cheerfully at the

thought.] *They might have lived together somewhere in Silver Town before Ordinance Road – I don't know. Her first husband was a bastard to her. He'd beat her all over the place.*

Around the time of John's fifth birthday, West Ham started the 1949/50 season in Division Two. The London docks, which spread out west from Canning Town, had been crippled by a dispute that had resulted in 13,000 dockers withdrawing their labour for over three weeks. The Labour Prime Minister, Clement Attlee, had condemned the action that left half the ships in the Port of London idle and unloaded. But the rationing of chocolates and confectionery had finally ended, so John, his brothers and sisters and the other children of the area, could go to the confectioners and buy as many sweets as they wanted, as long as they had the money of course. But overall, rationing was even more severe than in 1945.

The ravages of wartime bombing obliged whole sections of the population to take up residence in 'prefabs' (including the Redknapp family in the East End). These prefabricated homes were production line, factory-built houses, which were essentially boxes with flat roofs made of asbestos. Although the worst of wartime austerity had passed, John's family, like so many others in East London at that time, still needed to watch its finances:

My dad was quite a big man, he was very strict. I can remember my mum buying a brand new pair of shoes off the tally man. In them days we all made bikes or scooters from all the old scrap, bits and pieces. I was on this bike with these brand new shoes on and the pedals had spikes on 'em. They just ripped me shoes off completely. Me mum had to hide them till the following week till the tallyman came round again and sorted it out. But I got a belting for it. The old man used to take his belt off, cos he was a pretty big man and working in them docks and everything! He always said that he hit us with his belt because it would have been worse if he'd hit us with his hand. He could be heavy-handed.

Opposite page

Top left: 'That's me brother [Bonzo, behind John on right] and them two lived next door to me in Ordinance Road. Can you see my little girl's costume?' John laughed. 'Ah dear, talk about hard-up. That was at Southend – a day out or something, charabanc. I was about five then, in 1949. They used to live right bang next door, they did. They were the Youngs. They were brothers, and they had an older sister. The older boy, he only lived till he was eighteen, nineteen; he died of leukaemia.'

Top right: Little John.

Bottom left: John – already going places.

Bottom right: Father and son – John is with Moister Leopold.

Left: John Charles, young bear-back rider. *Right:* John and his sister Rita in uniform.

For all this, John had no notion of being part of a poor family or even an impoverished district:

> *I've got a photograph here somewhere and there's one car in the street. One car!* [He laughed incredulously.] *So no-one worried about money yer know, we were glad just to have our bit of grub and go out and play football. Everybody was in the same boat. The rationing was still going of course. We used to take the old ration book over to our corner shop for half of lard or whatever.*

It was then eleven peacetime seasons since West Ham had played in the top flight. Including the war period, the Hammers had not played in Division One, which was then the top flight of English football, for nineteen years. As the new decade of the fifties dawned, only a handful of people at the club could even remember those days. Certainly it meant little to John as he entered full-time education.

> *My primary school was Clarkson Street. That was down Rathbone Street and just round the corner to us. I was the only black kid in my school. There was*

no problems with that. None at all. I left there, cos they were going to knock it down, then I went to Star Lane and did me last year at primary school there where all me mates were. There were no black kids there other than my family. I didn't see any Asians when I was at school. I don't know what happened, me and me sister Rita and a feller a couple of doors away, who was round our house the other day as it happens, just before Christmas, Brian Walker, he brought all our fruit and veg' in, he's got his own firm at Spittlefields. He went to St Lukes, which was just round the corner to my school, Clarkson. I went to Clarkson Street, me sister went to Clarkson Street and all the rest of the kids except Brian in my turning went to Star Lane, but we don't know why. It wasn't because we was black, because Brian Walker wasn't black; I don't know why that happened. So I was happy to get to Star Lane because all me mates was there. I loved it at school. It was great!

The excitement generated by football in those grey years after the war is hard to conceptualise from the modern perspective and as John worked his way through school he too was infected with as much enthusiasm as most other boys in the area:

At Clarkson Street School, at play time, we used to have a ball out there and there was like toilets at the back of the playground and the kids used to try and kick the ball over there. I was one of the only boys who could kick the ball over the wall. I used to be able to belt it over there, you know. After school we'd all go home and have our tea, bread pudding or something like that and then we used to go over the debris at the back of our houses, bombsites. We'd pull up turfs of grass and make the goals and we'd play football until it got dark. We used to do that every single night. I never did any part-time work when I was at school. I never worried about money in them days, cos no-one had any.

John Charles had become conscious of football at the very start of the fifties and played his bombsite matches as the game entered its modern era. In 1950, Portsmouth and Wolves had finished level in Division One on 53 points, but Pompey took the title with a better goal average. Arsenal, with the Compton brothers and Joe Mercer, met Liverpool in the FA Cup Final. The Gunners took the trophy with a 2-0 victory. Reg Lewis scored both goals.

Sheffield Wednesday went into Division One with Spurs. Wednesday, with a goal average of 1.395, edged out their neighbours United, whose average was 1.387. West Ham finished the 1949/50 season just 4 points clear of relegation, finishing 2 points ahead of QPR. Plymouth and Bradford were dismissed from Division Two.

As the decade of war gave way to the mid-century, West Ham were not yet a club on the rise, but another more ominous 'team' was developing in the East End. In 1950, a sixteen-year-old Hackney boy called Harvey was found badly beaten up by fists, boots and bicycle chains. There were witnesses, but when the Kray twins, who were about the same age as Harvey, were put on trial at the Old Bailey, which was their debut at that venue, the case was dismissed because of lack of evidence.

Camping in the 1950s.

Football, like most other forms of mass entertainment, was cheap and accessible at that time. Match programmes in those days were 2d for 4 pages. A seat in the stand was 5s. After the game you could get a good seat in the cinema for less. *Take Me Out to the Ball Game* with Frank Sinatra, Gene Kelly and Esther Williams and *The Sands of Iwo Jima* starring John Wayne were pulling them in at the pictures. This gave substance to the dreams of the young people of the East End – the likes of Terrance Stamp for instance, would try to emulate these Hollywood stars.

At the start of the second half of the twentieth century, boys from the kind of background that John Charles came from were still able to identify with the men who turned out for West Ham. For John, one particular Hammer was influential:

> *I always supported and followed West Ham. I went with some boys who used to live over the back to me. I forget their names now. They took me to me first game and I think it was a reserve game. Then I can remember going to see the first team play. I used to watch Andy Malcolm. I liked watching Andy Malcolm. He was a tough little bugger. I liked him! I can always remember when he was marking Johnny Haynes. Johnny Haynes was captain of England and Andy just sort of chewed him up like. He was brilliant, Andy. He was a proper gentleman, but he was as tough as old boots. Was he hard!* [John shook his head and smiled in awe.]

When football resumed after the Second World War, West Ham was one of the first clubs to introduce a youth system to develop 'home-grown' talent. Another club to the forefront of youth football was Manchester United, and the introduction of the 'Busby Babes' was one of the classic stories of English soccer history. Such was the renown gained in local competition by the Old Trafford youngsters, they were prime favourites to win the FA Youth Cup when it was first inaugurated in 1952/53. This expectation proved to be well founded, as United won the first 4 finals.

In the spring of 1953, Everest had been climbed. In June, Queen Elizabeth II was crowned at Westminster Abbey and in the autumn, the guns of the Korean War had scarcely fallen silent when the rumbles of a new conflict began. The North Vietnamese, under their charismatic leader, Ho Chi Minh, were making life difficult for the colonial French. The tough French legionnaires and paratroopers who were sent to police the then French colony were accustomed to winning pitched battles where firepower and weapon superiority could be brought to bear, but the shadowy hit-and-run guerrilla tactics of their opponents puzzled and irritated the Europeans.

Football in England had less threatening irritations. In order to create a Saturday clear of League fixtures for the 1954 FA Cup Final, the scheduled programme of games for 1 May 1954 was brought forward to August 1953. West Ham's rearranged match was against Lincoln City on Wednesday 19 August. This was the first time since 1914, apart from the unusual circumstances of 1934/35, when the Hull City ground was closed on the first day of the season, that the Hammers had opened a season on any day other than a Saturday. The Boleyn boys beat Lincoln 5-0, which was the best start to a season the club had ever made.

Notts County came to Upton Park on 5 December 1953, but despite John Dick's fifth goal of the season, the Irons lost to the side that would, at the end of the season, finish in fourteenth position in Division Two, a place below West Ham. John's role model and inspiration during his early footballing days, Andy Malcolm, played his first game for West Ham that day. He was twenty years old, but had already been with the club for three years, having played 82 Reserve team games. He was one of the best wing-halves to don the claret and blue. He was strong, tough and even ruthless at times, but with a skill level rarely bestowed on the warrior class of his type. Andy personified West Ham's early commitment to developing local youth. He captained England schoolboys and was the Hammers' first youth international. Malcolm also played for the Football League in 1959. Often described as a feared wing-half with the ability to close-mark and block out opponents, he was able, almost instinctively, to snuff out the likes of Johnny Haynes, Jimmy Greaves and Dennis Law.

West Ham's youth policy began to show fruit during the 1953/54 term. In the second season of the FA Youth Cup, the Hammer's kids reached the semi-finals.

In 1955 John moved on to secondary school:

Me and my sister, Rita, went to Pretoria Road School. Rita must have been the only black girl there. But it was never mixed there. It was boys this end and girls that end. John Roberts, the head, was in charge of West Ham Boys. A lot of good players went to Pretoria – Alan Sealey, Frank Lampard. Me and another lad, Peter Turner (who was at Faraday School) were asked to visit Southampton. We went and had a look, but it was too far.

The West Ham Boys team was a good side. We used to win everything. We made the English School's Cup Final in 1959/60, but were thrashed 6-1 by

West Ham United, 1953/54. From left to right, back row: E. Devlin, T. Dixon, C. Newman, D. Bing, T. Standley, P. Chiswick, E. Gregory, G. Taylor, B. Rhodes, E. Armstrong, M. Musgrove, J. Barrett. Second row: T. Woodgate, D. Parker, M. Lill, P. Burdon, H. Gunning, D. McGowan, F. O'Farrell, N. Cantwell, G. Johnstone, A. Malcolm, D. Wragg, T. Matthews, A. Blackburn. Third row: E. Fuller (maintenance), D. Woodards (assistant groundsman), W. Robinson (junior coach), W. Moore (trainer), G. Wright, J. Belcher, F. Cooper, K. Brown, R. Walker, M. Allison, G. Gazzard, W. Nelson, J. Dick, H. Kinsell, H. Hooper (assistant trainer), W. St Pier (chief representative), A. Izatt (groundsman), H. Butler (assistant trainer). Front row: E.B.A. Fenton (manager), L.C. Cearns (vice-chairman), W.F. Cearns (director), A. Noakes, T. Southren, K. Tucker, A. Foan, E. Chapman, R.H. Pratt JP (chairman), D. Sexton, F. Kearns, J. Bond, H. Hooper, J. Andrews, Dr O. Thomas JP (director), C. Paynter (ambassador-at-large), F.H. Cearns (secretary).

Manchester. I was picked for Essex and London Boys. I went to England trials too. I did win five Youth caps for England in the end and we won the Junior World Cup – three lions on me chest. [John chuckled.]

This was a good West Ham Boys side – a very good side indeed. In fact, for most of the 1950s they were unbeaten, winning match after match from the Under-11s onward. It was the basis on which John was to claim international recognition. Although some have expressed that it was prejudice that probably robbed him of a schoolboy Cap, John was to become the first black player to represent England at any level, but he did not seem conscious of this point. When I put it to him he said simply, 'Yeah, I suppose I must have been.'

The school testimonial that John was given when he left full-time education shows that his attendance was exceptional. He told me, 'It had to be, I had to get me dinner.' He giggled. 'Free meals won it. One of my teachers, Smithy, was a bastard. He liked me though, I used to run and get his fags for him.'

John certainly remembered his school days with affection and he seemed to be a good student. The same school testimonial states, 'His work is neat, careful and intelligent. Well up to standard…top six in the class. Honest and trustworthy. Willing.' It was written by John Smith.

John, reflecting on the colour profile of his school, commented, 'I never had any black friends, in my little area there was hardly any there.' John's wife, Carol, added, 'There was only him.' John went on, 'I grew up and the black kids then were all them little flash ones. I remember one other black lad on the football scene at the time, Ernie Mackenzie. He played for South London Schoolboys, but he never made it into League football.'

It was shortly after this that John and his family moved to a home adjacent to the original domicile of West Ham United: 'When I was twelve or thirteen we moved to Ronald Avenue, which was right bang next to the Memorial Grounds. Our house was a big corner house, it was like a caretaker's house, or something like that. It was a big 'un. I was there up to '63. That was when we got married.'

'Parting with the ball is alright – but it is knowing when to part with it which can be so vital to a team.'

(*The Strategy of Soccer* – Johnny Byrne)

Three friends are in combat. Bobby Moore and Charlo put a double shadow on Spurs' super poacher, East Ham boy James Peter Greaves.

County Borough of West Ham

EDUCATION DEPARTMENT

TESTIMONIAL

Pretoria County Secondary Boys' School

Pretoria Road, London, E.16.

13th April, 1960

TO WHOM IT MAY CONCERN

John Charles - d/b. 20/9/44 - Form 4 A.

John Charles has attended this school regularly and punctually since September, 1956, and leaves in the top "A" class, 4.

His school work is neat, careful and intelligent, and well up to standard, and he is in the top section in the class.

He is thoroughly honest and trustworthy and is a cheerful, willing, and very well-mannered boy of excellent conduct.

As a result, he is very popular with boys and masters in this school and in West Ham.

He has shewn great ability at sport and has played cricket for the school, for West Ham, and for Essex. At football he has played for the school, for West Ham (where he is a great favourite), for Essex and for London. He was also chosen to go with the London boys to play against Berlin in Germany. He played in the first England trial and in the England v the Rest trial.

We are sure that he will make a sound, reliable employee, and can recommend him with pleasure and confidence.

Class Teacher ...*John Smith*... Head Teacher ...*JRoberts*...

A good scholar.

John and Carol cut the cake.

3

West Ham Boys

'Practise with the ball from an early age and keep on at it even though at times you might feel fed up with it all...glamour follows learning of the arts...draw another defender, and open up a gap in the middle...learn to control the ball at speed. Once your man is beaten – move on.'

(The Strategy of Soccer – Johnny Byrne)*

I have devoted this chapter to the memories and views of two of John's oldest friends, Charlie Green, who is now a successful businessman based in Essex, and Reg Lerseurf. They are former members of the most successful West Ham Boys teams ever and one of the outstanding district schoolboy sides of the fifties. Outside of his family, these two men probably know more about John's early years than any living person. The three, Chas, Reg and John, remained firm friends for almost half a century after they first joined forces to make the young Hammers a feared and respected side wherever kids kicked a football throughout England's green and pleasant land.

Charlie Green was born in Stratford and moved to Forest Gate. He told me: 'I went to Stratford Green School. I could go into a school and get any member of the West Ham team out of school for the day. I just went up to the Headmaster and told him there was training. They never phoned up to find out, but I don't think they had phones in them days.'

Reg interjected, 'He was like a king. He used to sit in the playground in a chair. I was at Harold Road School, and I had to go to Stratford Green for the football, which was about an hour's journey in them days, so it was an hour there and an hour back – the afternoon was gone!'

Charlie: 'We played together as West Ham Boys and it was kinda like a trio. We stayed mates and always kept in touch. I used to go over the Memorial Grounds when I was like twelve. I used to go on me bike from Forest Gate. I could have played football with me mates locally, but I went over there just to play football with John's mates and him. Little Clive [John's younger brother] used to come out with us. That's how we met and how I got to know the family. I made the journey because we were mates. That's what you did for yer mates! Me fondest memories were when we were kids over the Memorial. Going round John's house. I loved his family and he liked my mum and dad as well. Playing with little Clive, when he learnt to kick a ball. That's what I want to remember forever.'

Reg added, 'But if you wanted a decent game that's where you'd go. My first memory of John was playing with him at school. John was always outgoing, but not leary.'

Charlie continued: 'John's mum used to cook a lot. She used to feed me. She was lovely, his mum, she was a cracker. Something else, she was lovely. And of course, the girls. When I went to Charlo's funeral I've gone over to Margaret, one of John's sisters. I said, "Hallo Margaret." She says, "Hello." I said, "You don't remember me, do yer?" She said, "No." I said, "It's Charlie Green." She never said hallo or anything! [Charlie guffawed.] She says, "You were a bleeder when you were young!" What a nice thing to say! No. They are a lovely family. He was lucky, John. My sister was a lot older than me, still is. I met Johnnie when I was playing for Stratford Green and he was playing for Pretoria. Schoolboy football. When you played for West Ham Boys in the late fifties it meant that you couldn't play for your school team on the Saturday, but you didn't have a West Ham Boys team more than once every two or three weeks, so you were always playing against yer mates. We had an elite allegiance to each other in that boys team.'

Reg: 'We were closer than most teams. John didn't play for the eleven-year-olds, but he was involved. I knew him from secondary school. We all came into it together when we were in the twelves.'

Charlie: 'We were a little bit special to each other, even on the pitch we protected each other like bloody mad.'

Reg: 'Most of the teams we played in before or after weren't the same, but they didn't have the success we did. We only lost one game in years, that final against Manchester.'

Charlie: 'One game in all them years!'

Reg: 'That was from twelve right the way through to fifteen. Going back to Under-11s we never lost all the way through. That takes some doing yer know!' He shook his head. 'The only game we lost was at West Ham, under the floodlights, to Manchester Boys. The only game me mum and dad come to see me play and we lost 6-1. I never spoke to them again after that.' We all laughed but Charlie remained poker faced. He is a born comedian and loves the role of a sort of cockney Bob Hope. Reg continued, 'There was a lot of friendship.'

Charlie: 'Don't forget that in one year, out of us eleven, eight of us played for Essex and that takes some doing. Essex included West Ham, East Ham, Ilford, Havering. There were at least twelve good teams in Essex, that's well over one hundred players and eight of our West Ham team played for Essex.' Reg recalled that game when eight of West Ham's finest took the field together, 'I remember we got beat by Middlesex. Ronnie Harris was playing for them and we lost 5-4. It was mud! Chas and John played for London. I never played for London.' Charlie insisted, 'We played on Ipswich's ground, the only time we played at Portman Road. Sometimes we used to play over Temple Mills. The pitch was on the top of a rubbish tip.'

Reg: 'It always seemed to be cold and windy over there, and raining.' According to Charlie, John Charles was 'the best defender in the country as a schoolboy'. He turned to Reg and put a hand on his shoulder and said, 'You were good too, Reg.'

Reg smiled at me, accepting the comic condescension and added, 'John was brave. You had to have respect for John too. There was this bloke, Tony Cardoza. John had fluid on the knee, he'd get that quite often. He wasn't playing this day because of that,

John with Dave Bickles – future 'Boleyn Boys'.

but he was around. Anyway, for some reason, John's taken umbrage towards Cardoza. He's walked in the dressing room and said, "You Tony Cardoza?" Cardoza says, "Yes", and Johnnie's hit him with a left – bang! Cardoza's said "I'll get my brother on to you." I said to him, "Tony, don't bother. His brothers are bigger than yours." But I had to stop John or he'd have killed Cardoza. John was about fifteen at the time and it was just as he was leaving school. It was probably one of our last schoolboy games. He could be a hard git. Brian Dear used to put it about a bit. He'd try it with people like Dave Bickles, but Dave wouldn't have none of it. Dave was as strong as an ox. Brian would take it out on me. He'd never try it on with John.'

Charlie confirmed John's pugilistic qualities: 'I was in a bundle with John. It was down at the Two Puddings – upstairs. We were up there discoing. My cousin was a bouncer there. Someone was taking the piss out of one of us, it was one of the first discos up there to have ultraviolet lights, and you could see his dandruff. John could have a fight!'

'Full control is essential.... Where all players can aid the team ... is by helping each other ... be conscious of an immediate opponent.'

(*The Strategy of Soccer* – Johnny Byrne)

4

I Wanted to be a
Lorry Driver's Mate

'I hate to see a player make a really telling pass and then lean back and admire his handiwork. Defeat this attitude early in life. Always be ready to fight to the bitter end.'

(The Strategy of Soccer – Johnny Byrne)

At the end of September 1957, one of the worst confrontations between blacks and whites in the civil rights struggle in the United States took place in the southern state of Arkansas. A federal district court order had decreed that nine black students should be admitted to the previously segregated Central High School in the town of Little Rock. However, the segregationist Governor of Arkansas, Orville Faubus, took every possible step to prevent the students being enrolled at the school, including mobilising the National Guard to bar the doors on them. At President Eisenhower's insistence, the Guard was finally withdrawn, but its place was taken by a white mob that continued to keep the black students out. In an extraordinary move, the President sent 1,000 army paratroopers to Little Rock and removed the National Guard from Faubus' control. Only with this military escort could the nine black children enter the school.

1957 – West Ham's first FA Youth Cup final: baptism of fire
In 1957 the Irons made their first appearance in the FA Youth Cup final and became the first southern club to achieve that distinction. They faced Manchester United. The first leg took place at Upton Park and a crowd of 15,000 turned up to cheer on the claret and blue progeny that included the full-back Joe Kirkup, who would help West Ham win the European Cup Winners Cup in 1965. The future Hammers manager, John Lyall, who would steer his club to FA Cup glory one day, was also in the line-up.

West Ham took the lead through Johnny Cartwright (who was destined to become a coach in the England set up) in the 22nd minute; however, less than a quarter of an hour later, the Red Devil's centre forward kept up his remarkable record of scoring in every tie in the tournament by grabbing the equaliser. 2 goals in five minutes just after the break saw United take a firm grasp on the final, but with just over an hour played, the Hammers forward George Fenn pulled his side back into the tie.

Despite a spirited performance, West Ham were left with a lot to do at Old Trafford five days later. A crowd of 23,000 cheered in 2 goals apiece for Mike Pearson and Alex

JOHN CHARLES
...Not, of course, THE
John Charles but a West
Ham schoolboy footballer
who is already making
his mark in the game
Picture by Robert Stiggins.

'Go, go, go Johnnie go'...Charlo is honing his skills on the Memorial Grounds, Canning Town (Canning Town gasworks are in the background).

Dawson (making 21 scored in ten games) and another from the left-winger, Reg Hunter, that enabled United to retain the trophy. Dawson was later to be seen attacking West Ham's goal for Preston in the 1964 Cup final.

It was at this point that the first true sadness came into John's life:

My dad was a lot older than my mum. He started having trouble with his eyes after we moved from Ordinance Road. Eventually he went blind. The first time I really wanted to hit anyone was when the council sent a bloke round my house to help me dad, a man who'd been working in the docks with his hard hands and everything like that, and he's gone blind and this bloke gave him a Braille book. And I thought, 'How can my dad bloody well do that?' I felt like smashing that bloke. We just slung it, the book, soon as he went and that was that. Dad was sixty-seven when he died, I was fourteen.

It was during this difficult period that John got his first chance to break into professional sport, but the offer was not for football, 'I was a pretty good cricketer. Essex phoned up when me dad died. I couldn't go and play for them because me father died.' The loss for Essex would be West Ham's gain.

The world of football was rocked on 6 February 1958, when eight Manchester United players were among the twenty-one passengers killed in an air crash in West Germany.

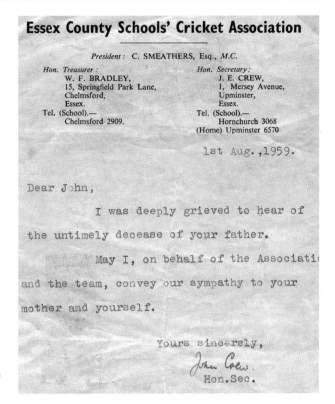

Essex County Schools' Cricket Association

President : C. SMEATHERS, Esq., *M.C.*

Hon. Treasurer :
W. F. BRADLEY,
15, Springfield Park Lane,
Chelmsford,
Essex.
Tel. (School).—
Chelmsford 2909.

Hon. Secretary :
J. E. CREW,
1, Mersey Avenue,
Upminster,
Essex.
Tel. (School).—
Hornchurch 3068
(Home) Upminster 6570

1st Aug. ,1959.

Dear John,

I was deeply grieved to hear of the untimely decease of your father.

May I, on behalf of the Associati and the team, convey our sympathy to your mother and yourself.

Yours sincerely,

John Crew.
Hon.Sec.

Essex lose John Charles, West Ham gain Charlo.

The accident happened as the aeroplane was taking the United team back to Manchester from Yugoslavia. They had just drawn with Red Star Belgrade to qualify for the semi-final of the European Cup. Their aeroplane failed to clear a fence on take-off from Rhiem airport in Munich. Among the dead were the English regulars Roger Byrne, Duncan Edwards and Tommy Taylor. United's manager, Matt Busby, was also seriously injured. The aeroplane, a BEA Ambassador, was reduced to a tangled heap of wreckage. Driving snow hampered rescue workers.

Shortly after one of football's worst ever tragedies, the team that had averaged thirteenth place in Division Two throughout the fifties, scoring less than 67 goals a season, would, during the 1957/58 campaign, score 111 League and Cup goals and take the Championship. West Ham clinched promotion and the Division Two title in their final game of the season, when they won at Middlesbrough. In the process John Dick scored the 100th claret-and-blue League goal of the season.

West Ham were welcomed back to Division One at Portsmouth on 23 August 1958. 7,000 of the 40,000 crowd were Hammers fans, which was a very high number of travelling supporters in those days. They went into raptures when Keeble and Dick scored to start West Ham off with a win.

The next day, troubles flared up after five black men were beaten up by white youths in Notting Hill in north-west London. The police made more than 150 arrests during three days of serious rioting. On the night of 30 August, some 200 white and black people fought in the streets. Property was damaged and one black household was petrol-bombed. The following evening saw some of the worst disturbances, with four hours of continuous running battles between 400 people. During this conflict, police were attacked and injured. On 1 September, gangs of up to 2,000 youths and children attacked houses where black people lived, breaking windows and causing extensive damage. Police suspected the involvement of extreme political groups.

1959 – West Ham's second FA Youth Cup Final: Smillie's people

The spring of 1959 saw the Hammers make another appearance in the final of the FA Youth Cup, having eliminated the Arsenal youngsters in the last four. They faced a strong Blackburn Rovers side, who had accounted for Manchester United in the semi-final. In the claret-and-blue defence that day, was the young Bobby Moore, Harry Cripps – who would become a favourite at Millwall's Den and the stalwarts of the future West Ham side, Jack Burkett and Eddie Bovington. However, the Irons could only manage 1-1 in the first game at Upton Park. Andy Smillie scored for the Hammers whilst Rovers put the ball through the legs of the West Ham 'keeper, Caskey.

In the second leg, West Ham held Rovers at 0-0 over ninety minutes, but because of the level aggregate score, were obliged to play extra time. The young Irons had run their opponents ragged over the two matches, but the best team did not win. Blackburn scored the only goal at Ewood Park. Fred Pickering, who went on to play for Everton and England, had captained the Rovers side in both games.

As the fifties gave way to the sixties, the price of a ticket at Upton Park was amongst the highest in the country, but the fans were, after many years, getting some return for their money. In the final home game of the 1958/59 season, the Hammers beat Manchester City 5-1 to finish in sixth place in Division One, just two points behind third-placed Arsenal, whom West Ham had defeated at Highbury in March. This was the best League perfor-mance by the Hammers in their forty-year history in the competition. It would remain the best until John Lyall's Irons, with the likes of Phil Parkes, Alan Devonshire and Tony Cottee, took third place in 1986. However, the 1959 West Ham scored more goals than Lyall's lads (85 to 74). Ted Fenton, who had occupied a managerial role at the Boleyn Ground since 1950 and who had been associated with the club from his boyhood days, with a deal of help from the likes of Malcolm Allison, Noel Cantwell and John Bond, had brought the Hammers into a new era of football at Upton Park. Promotion had been the start of West Ham's golden years that would culminate in the mid-sixties.

At the end of a satisfying campaign, many West Ham supporters would have seen the lavish screen version of George Gershwin's black folk opera, *Porgy and Bess*, that summer. The film won the Oscar for best scoring of a musical. Set in the slums of Catfish Row in South Carolina, it tells the tragic love story of the crippled beggar, Porgy (Sidney Poitier) and the beautiful, reckless Bess (Dorothy Dandridge). The stage version was first launched in New York by the Theatre Guild in 1935.

18 June saw violent disturbances in the South African city of Durban. Days of serious rioting were sparked off when police destroyed illicit stills during a slum clearance operation designed to resettle some 100,000 black people. Hundreds of black women attacked beer-halls and other property in the black shantytown of Cato Manor on the

Fred Pickering in his Blackpool
incarnation.

outskirts of Durban. They were joined by thousands of other rioters who ran through
the streets setting fire to offices, clinics, schools, shops and vehicles. Outside Durban,
a crowd of some 4,000 blacks blocked the main road and stoned cars as they tried to
pass. The rioting continued throughout the month, leaving buildings and vehicles
smouldering. Four black people died in the unrest, and damage to property was
estimated at some £250,000. The situation in Durban remained tense for some months
afterwards and more deaths occurred in September when police opened fire on
protesters.

During the autumn and winter that followed, John began to move into his vocation.
Following the club's first sighting of John by Ernie Gregory, John told how:

*Walley St Pier, the chief coach at West Ham at the time, used to follow our team.
We hadn't lost a game and he was getting interested in a few of the players.
Before one game a teacher told us that a West Ham scout was there and to do
our best when we went out there to play. Me and Reg Le Seurf, who was a good
friend of mine – he went to Harold Road School, were asked to come for a trial
at Cumberland Road. It was organised by Walley St Pier. After that Walley came
up to me and said, 'I'm ever so pleased that you played today and I'd like to
have you down at West Ham. Come and join us on the books'. I wasn't well
pleased. I went home and told me mum and she had to go with me up the
school because I didn't want to go to West Ham, I wanted to be a lorry driver's*

The men who started the 'Academy' and invented the modern English game. From left to right, back row: Dave Sexton (who would manage Chelsea), John Bond (who managed several top clubs), Ernie Gregory (West Ham's longest serving employee), Malcolm Allison (the boss of, amongst others, Manchester City and Crystal Palace), Noel Cantwell (the Irish international, who would become manager of Coventry City), Frank O'Farrell (who captained Eire and was the top man at Leicester and Manchester United). Front row: Malcolm Musgrove (who coached at many clubs and was assistant manager at Old Trafford), Harry Hooper (the England international), Billy Dare, John Dick (the Scottish international) and Ken Tucker.

mate. [John laughed at the thought.] *I'm glad I didn't.* [He chuckled again.] *The kids who took me to West Ham, they were older than me and that's what they were doing. They were lorry driver's mates getting about £2, £2.50 a week. But I went to West Ham straight from school. It was Christmas 1959.*

John reflected on the fate of football:

Other players at that trial were Charlie Green and Peter Turner – Peter sat next to me in school. He went to all the England trials. He got in, I didn't. He played for England Boys at Wembley, but he went to Arsenal. He was only at Arsenal for about a year before they let him go. Me boy gave me some old West Ham v. Arsenal programmes and Peter Turner was in one of them. It had appearance records and he only had the one, so he couldn't have done all that well. Now if he'd have come to West Ham I think he might have got on a little bit better. Reg Le Seurf joined West Ham the same time as me. He became an electrician over West Ham and done all the lights. That's strange ain't it, coming to play football and the next time you see him he's up there on the floodlights. [John chortled softly. He raised his eyebrows remembering.] *Kenny Lynch's brother Mel was in the youth side, but never made the first team.* [Kenny was to be John's lifelong friend.]

When John joined the Upton Park staff he soon forgot his lorry-driving ambitions:

My attitude changed when I actually got into West Ham and started training and everything. On my first day I sowed the seeds on the pitch. I cleaned all the stand out, scrubbed it out, washed it out, painted it, that's what we had to do. Paint the ground before you even kicked a ball. You didn't kick a ball until all that work was done. Underneath the stands stencilling 'A' block, 'B' block, all that and that's what I did. The groundsman was in charge of us. George Isaacs his name was. George had that where all yer hair falls out, alopecia. To hide his head he had this cap. No-one ever saw him without this cap on. One day we was all up in the stands painting and old George was on the tractor cutting the grass. Then all of a sudden I heard someone shouting 'It's off! It's off!' I turned round and Roger Hugo [who was to make the professional ranks at West Ham] *was shouting, 'The fucking hat's off!* [John tittered.] *'It's off!' And when I've*

Albert Walker (trainer with the ball), next to him the club secretary, Eddie Chapman, then Walley St Pier, head scout. Front row: JC, Mick Beesley, Ron Boyce, Peter Brabrook, Roger Hugo, John Starkey, Martin Peters, Reg Leseurf. Back row: Brian Dear, Frank Caskey (almost hidden), Eddie Presland, Dave Bickles.

*looked it was frightening cos his bald head was pure, pure white! If he'd have
let it go with the weather, you know, it would have looked alright.* [He laughed
again.] *But he wore this cap for so many years on his head…it was pure white!*

When John arrived at the Boleyn Ground, there were a few other faces around that
would be familiar in the future: 'Some of the lads, like John Lyall, worked in the office.
Brian Dear was on the ground staff with me. Boycey (Ronnie Boyce) had just signed
pro' and Martin Peters was around.'

The life of a young football apprentice was not easy and the pay was not fantastic:
'When I was a pro' I went and worked in Dagenham on the A13 in a rubber glove
factory. They used to give me a nice little wage packet at the end of the week that made
up me other wage from West Ham. Nice!'

But if the youngsters had to work hard they seemed to make sure they had some
compensation, 'Outside of football I used to like a drink. We used to go out – Dave
Bickles, Deary [Brian Dear] and me.' However, like all things in life, we pay for our joys,
especially when they inextricably become the source or expression of our pain.

'To be caught in "no man's land" must be a goalkeeper's nightmare, for it does
so much to pass the initiative to the opposing player or players.'

(The Strategy of Soccer – Johnny Byrne)

Above: Poetry in motion: Martin Peters.

Opposite left: Charlo and Dave Bickles are warming up for a traditional Dutch game of 'foot-basket'.

Opposite right: Where is everyone? Charlo is at the Upton Park of the past.

5

The Dawn of the Sixties

'Skill without fitness is like chips without fish.'

(The Strategy of Soccer – Johnny Byrne)

As the new decade opened the Cold War was in full swing, and many people thought a nuclear confrontation with the Soviet Union was a distinct possibility. In March, what had begun as a peaceful protest ended in tragedy in the South African township of Sharpville, when police opened fire on a black crowd, killing sixty-seven people and wounding 186. The shootings happened on a day of mass demonstrations against the white government's hated pass-laws. In a campaign organised by the Pan-African Congress, a breakaway group from the African National Congress, black people all over the country left their passes at home and gave themselves up at their nearest police station to be arrested. Thousands took part in the protests, which were peaceful in the majority of places. However, at Sharpeville, five miles north of Vereeniging, police officers confronted the crowd outside the police station and opened fire, apparently without warning. Official statements claimed that the shootings took place in self-defence when the crowd of 20,000 tried to storm the station. Black witnesses at the subsequent inquiry said that only 5,000 people were involved and that they had gone peacefully to the police station to discuss the pass laws. A medical expert testified that some seventy per cent of the victims had been shot from behind.

Record Retailer, which was to become *Music Week,* began its 'Top 40' in March 1960. The first number one demonstrated the change in popular music taste since the early fifties. It was a pouting, moody, Jimmy Dean clone – Adam Faith with *Poor Me.* This was overtaken a week later by *Running Bear,* rendered by Johnny Preston. A skiffle icon and one of the best guitarists ever to strum a string, Lonnie Donegan took over at the end of March with what was to become, alas, an enduring cockney anthem, *My Old Man's a Dustman.* Soon the North Bank at Upton Park were adding it to the growing repertoire that, apart from *I'm Forever Blowing Bubbles*, included *The Hokey-Cokey* and the perennial *Knees Up Muvver Brown.* Anthony Newley was next to top the charts with *Do You Mind?* At the same time Adam Faith came straight in at number three with *Someone Else's Baby*.

Towards the end of the 1959/60 term, West Ham had played some good football, but over the season 91 goals were scored against them. They had lost 16 games after November and only managed 1 win in the final 8 matches. This meant that they finished

From left to right: Harry Redknapp, Brian Dear, John Sissons, Billy Bonds, John Charles, after a training run with some of the local youth.

in fourteenth place, just 4 points clear of relegated Leeds. This was a disappointing end to their campaign after being top of the League early on. Aston Villa and Cardiff replaced the Peacocks of Leeds and bottom club Luton in Division One.

In November 1960, John F. Kennedy was elected as President of the USA. This opened a new era for America and world politics. Kennedy had a youthful approach, good looks and a broad appeal to many groups and communities, including America's black population. It was not long before the political Right in the US would see the threat posed to their interests by a Kennedy/Luther King and maybe even a post-Mecca Malcolm X partnership.

What looked like the start of one dynasty was followed by the end of another in East London. In March 1961, Ted Fenton left West Ham. It was not, and never has been, clear if Fenton resigned or if he had been sacked. He never commented on the affair, but it was rumoured that he had 'been allowed to resign'. Perhaps part of the reason was West Ham's second mediocre showing in Division One, where they finished in an unimpressive sixteenth place. However, Fenton had been responsible for bringing nearly all of the great West Ham players of the sixties to Upton Park. Many thought that Fenton was a permanent fixture at the club. In his eleven years as West Ham's manager, Ted had presided over the birth of a revolution in British football at the Boleyn Ground, although this was instigated by the young Malcolm Allison (see *Days of Iron*). At the same time he was one of the 'old school', a white-collar leader, wielding a pipe rather

Left: Adam Faith and Connie Francis.

Right: John is at Butlins, forming an interest in coaching. He never really liked any sport outside of football and confessed that, until he discovered gardening and cooking when he left the professional game, he had no hobbies, apart from 'sitting around in the most comfortable armchair that was available.'

Opposite: John, with everything still to play for.

than wearing a tracksuit. However, he brought something of the modern world to the club, particularly in terms of his relationship with the press and the fans. He was a man made in the English Second Division game of the 1930s and '40s.

Fenton moved on to take charge of Southend United. It has been forgotten or over-looked that Ted, Allison and the talent of scout Walley St Pier, who brought the likes of Peters, Moore, Hurst, Boyce and John Charles to the club, had laid the basis for the future. In that respect he may be thought of as West Ham's greatest manager, although naked statistics would give that honour to the incoming manager, Ron Greenwood, who built the foundations laid by Allison under the jurisdiction of Fenton.

Many supporters had been taken aback when an 'Arsenal man' (Greenwood had been assistant manager at Highbury) had been put in charge of the Irons. This situation was not helped by the rest of his life-history. He was a northerner. He had been part of the Chelsea side that won the Championship in 1955. He was the first West Ham manager not to have played for the club. All Ron's CV needed to make the picture

complete was a part-time job selling peanuts at White Hart Lane. However, John Charles knew that his new manager was not an Arsenal, Chelsea or, for that matter, a West Ham man. The most important thing for Ron was what he wanted and his standards. John recalled that 'Greenwood didn't like Andy Malcolm. He didn't like a lot of 'em that Ted Fenton got there. He wanted his own mob.'

For all this, Greenwood had worked with the England Youth and Under-23 teams. This, together with the fact that Ted Fenton had, with the help of Malcolm Allison, left Greenwood a decent legacy in terms of the potential of the team, gave cause for some optimism about the coming season.

In the first few weeks of 1962, the Soviet Union took the provocative step of reserving the air corridors between West Germany and West Berlin for use by only its own military planes. Their harassment of Western Aircraft heightened the tension as Bobby Moore scored the only goal of the Division One game at Stamford Bridge. By the end of March, Johnny Byrne had arrived at Upton Park from Crystal Palace for £65,000, which was an English record fee at the time. Greenwood knew the second-generation Irish lad through his work with the England Under-23 side, for whom Byrne had played with some distinction. Although a bit on the short side for a centre-forward, Byrne was a sleek and artful player, which was just the type of striker Greenwood admired. However, the cultured young player failed to make much of an impact during his first game, which was a goalless draw at Hillsborough, and he did not do much better on the social side of things in the first instance.

John's fellow West Ham Boys teammate, Charlie Green, told me, 'When we signed Budgie Byrne, the "grease monkey", he had Brylcream everywhere. We used to go in Ed's café over the road after training on a Wednesday night. It was six, seven o'clock at night. Everybody used to go in there, bacon sandwiches, sausage sandwiches, egg and chips. You all had to queue up, no matter if you played in the first team or the juniors or the A team, or the Reserves. Well, we're all lining up, there was a fair old queue that night and Budgie came in and went straight to the front of the queue! Well, that upset Johnnie – he gave him a mouthful and that put Budgie Byrne right to the back of the queue. Don't forget John was only a junior or a colt then. There was a big round of applause. [Charlie mimicked the cheering.] Raaay! That's the only time I ever see John really angry.'

However, Budgie and Charlo were soon to become firm friends and drinking companions and, by the end of April the situation on the pitch was looking up. At the Boleyn Ground, Alan Sealey, who had come to Upton Park from Orient in an exchange that had sent David Dunmore to Brisbane Road, picked up the rebound when Byrne hit the Cardiff City bar to score West Ham's first goal of the game in the fifty-third minute. With just seven minutes of the game left, from a tight angle Byrne scored his first goal as a Hammer. The game ended in a 4-1 win for the Irons.

In Greenwood's first complete term, West Ham had made an improvement of eight places on their First Division position of the previous season. Apart from Byrne, all the other big names of the campaign were already at the club when Ron arrived. However, Greenwood had brought a crop of youngsters into the first team squad, including Martin Peters, Alan Dickie, Jack Burkett and Ronnie Boyce, who, like Peters, was a local lad. Most of the side were East Enders – young men who had grown up in the youth team together and knew each other well.

The struggle for black civil rights in America reached a climax in 1963. Black rights workers were murdered in Alabama and Mississippi. In June, President Kennedy had to federalise the Alabama National Guard when George Wallace, the segregationist Governor of Alabama, tried to prevent two black students from taking up their places at the University of Alabama in Tuscaloosa. Peaceful protest marches in Birmingham, Alabama, were met by force and weeks of violent rioting ensued on the city's streets, with police using tear-gas and fire hoses to contain the situation. In September, a bomb killed four black schoolgirls in the city.

Before the new season opened there was a hint of things to come. The Hammers had won the American Challenge Cup in the USA, which was a tournament that took up most of the closed season. The Irons beat Dukla Prague in the final in Chicago, preventing them from completing a treble; they had won the Challenge Cup two years in succession. Dukla had seven of the Czech internationals on their side, including the European Footballer of the Year for 1962, Josef Masopust. The Czech national team were a formidable force. They had played six games during the 1962 World Cup in Chile. However, John was unable to take a share in the glory. His youngest son, Mitch, related how 'Brian Dear told me that when they went out to play in America in '63, Dad couldn't go. The club thought it best not to take him because of the problems out there with racism.'

Returning from the World Cup in Chile, Bobby Moore was in the West Ham side which found itself a Derek Dougan goal down within a minute of the 1962/63 season's first whistle at Villa Park. A couple of minutes later McEwan had the Irons chasing the game. Baker, Dougan and McEwan all bruised the Hammers' woodwork in the second half. West Ham lost 3-1.

On 28 August the wave of black protest in America crested in an enormous demonstration, when around 200,000 black and white civil rights supporters marched to Washington DC from all over the United States. The climax to the march came when the crowd gathered around the Lincoln Memorial. There they were addressed by Martin Luther King, who told them in a powerful and moving speech of his continuing dream of equality in America.

Brian Dear made his debut in the next game at Wolverhampton. 'Stag' was born in West Ham in 1943. He joined the club as a fifteen-year-old. He was a tussling, roustabout, buccaneering striker, whose style and skill was honed on the streets, playing fields and bombsites of East London. Wolves won their first game in four visits to Upton Park. This, alongside the opening match at Villa and, most disastrous of all, a 6-1 walloping from Spurs (John Lyall scored an own-goal) in front of 30,000 disappointed Upton Park fans, meant that West Ham started the season with three straight defeats.

As the sixties really began to swing and the gloom of the fifties was lifting, West Ham's John Charles came of football age, but he also made another big step in life:

In 1963 I signed pro. I was seventeen. I was married at eighteen. Carol was a mate of me sister, Rita – they worked together. I used to go round her house, she

John and Carol are having a drink with a couple of parrots early in the swinging sixties.

came round mine. Rita went out for a drink with her brother and his mates, I used to drink with Rita and that's how it happened. We were courting for about two years before we got married in St Matthias'.

Carol light-heartedly recalled, 'It was his arrogance. He just kept chasing me and in the end I went, "Alright".' John smiled, 'She used to follow me around.'

Carol: 'Don't write that, Brian – that was one load of old bullshit – he tells everyone I fell at his feet.' They both laughed. From the start of their relationship Carol had become part of West Ham's social cycle: 'I used to go to the reserves a lot with John's sister, Jan Dear, Brian Dear's mum and Dave Bickles' wife. We'd go with our mums and dads.'

John talked about his early experience of marriage and the social side of life at West Ham: 'We'd sometimes go to a pub or a meal.' Carol: 'We used to go to Jimmy's Steak House in Stratford every Saturday.'

We moved to 712 Barking Road – just round the corner to the Boleyn. Rob Jenkins, the physio, lived upstairs with his first wife, Unya, a Dutch girl she was. When we got married, Brian Dear and all them all had their girlfriends, Dave Bickles, we all used to go out, round my house or round Carol's, and we had a few parties at our flat, on the Barking Road. We came out of that flat cos it was Robby's dad's, Bill. He give it to us for three years. Then he let us have it for £4 a week. He said after a while he was going to put it up to £6. We said, 'You're joking! We can buy our own house for that!'

Right: 'The future's so bright they gotta wear shades.' John, Dave Bickles, Harry Cripps and Eddie Presland are on tour in Holland.

Below: John and Carol are out with the Bickles.

Our first mortgage was about £28 a month. We bought this place [John and Carol lived in a three-bedroomed, semi-detached house in Barkingside] *for £4,500 in 1966. It was all just fun. That was the sixties. Carol's brother used to come down every Thursday night and we'd go for a drink round the Black Lion* [Plaistow]. *We took the other John Charles in there once.* [This was the late Welsh giant and football genius who played for Juventus and Leeds United]. *It was after we played Leeds at home. We went to a party in Ronan Point, those were the flats that fell down – that was a couple of days after we were up there!*

The collapse of Ronan Point in Canning Town, which narrowly missed being a major disaster, seemed to mirror the state of things at Upton Park at the time. John turned professional during something of a crisis time for the Hammers. As the year turned, West Ham were at the very foot of Division One, having won just 6 games in 19 outings. 8 defeats were behind them, but John did not let that get in the way of his enjoyment of life. He told me:

We liked all the music. I liked anything that come out. When I was a kid it was all Frankie Laine, Bing Crosby, Ricky Nelson, Connie Francis and all that. I never liked all that reggae or calypso, none of that. Then Elvis Presley, Joe Brown, Peggy and Brenda Lee, and Billy Fury. We used to have a jive. I'd have Carol over me back, over me shoulder. [John and Carol giggled.] *Well…I couldn't sling her over me shoulder. We'd dance, jive and twist. I used to get up in the pubs and sing. I liked whatever was in the charts. We used to go dancing down the Lotus, off the Romford Road, Forest Gate, East Ham Town Hall; they'd get a group in. The Small Faces played there once and they chucked them off for being too loud. We'd go to the Central Pub. Brian Dear met Jan* [his wife] *in there, upstairs at the dance. We liked Adam Faith, Buddy Holly, those sort of singers. In fact me and old Dave Bickles used to like anything. Every Friday, as soon as we got our wages, we used to go and buy records with Brian Dear at this little record shop in East Ham. Deary* [Brian Dear] *knew it. They used to get all the up-to-date 45s or 78s. What was top of the pops at the time. The Beatles, Alma Cogan, Cliff Richard or whatever – there was no stress or worries then.*

Carol reminded John, 'You had that little red van didn't yer. It was like a GPO [General Post Office] van.'

John:'It was a Ford Thames van.'

Carol:'You used to get me and me mates all sitting in the back.'

John: 'The manager never said anything at all about us going out and stuff. We used to hide the cars but Ernie Gregory used to know, he was a bit cute and he was with us some of the time. He knew all our tricks; he'd done 'em himself.' John smiled.

John, who played centre-back at that time, captained West Ham's first Youth Cup winning side in 1963, and was the first black player to lead a first-class side to a major trophy.

Charlo and Carol with
first-born Keith and
newcomer Lesley.

The first leg of the final was played at Anfield. I was just eight years old and was one of a few hundred to make the journey to support West Ham's youngsters. I made the trip up to Liverpool with a group of mates and a couple of their bigger brothers. It seems fantastic today, when we are so careful about our young, and fearful of their fate. To state the obvious, attitudes then were not the same as they are today. L.P. Hartley maybe summed things up when he wrote [on the opening page of the Prologue to *The Go-Between*] 'The past is a foreign country: they do things differently there.'

It was a hellish journey though, all the way crushed with at least a dozen others in the back of a dilapidated 'Mr Cone-Head' ice-cream van. Even in its better days this 'winged carriage' had been no chariot of fire. As we entered Liverpool, the livery of our conveyance which before we had started out had been a celebration of the capacity of the sixties British paint industry's invention, and a homage to Dulux, had been enlivened by trails of multicoloured vomit, which could have been traced all the way back to London. As if we were not conspicuous enough, we decided to turn on the van's chimes 'for a laugh'. However, once they were dingling out, the manic strains would not turn off, so all the way around Liverpool we drew much unwanted attention with what seemed to me in my ignorance a rather jolly tune. It was in fact a merry version of the German National anthem. It turned out that Big Reg, our driver, who was 5ft 2in tall, and had been expelled from jockey school for trying to sell a thoroughbred to a group of amicable Romany horse-traders, was tone deaf. He had bought the chimes cheap from a bloke he had met in the public bar of the Black Lion Pub, Plaistow. This 'Tunemeister' called himself 'Hanzy'. Reg said that he had 'sounded like an Australian'. Hanzy had told Reg that the chimes were *Zar Teddy Bez's Pishnict.*

Amazingly, we got to the ground unmolested. In fact, as we parked our gaily coloured, singing, ringing transport, a scruffy little lad ran up and asked for a '99'. Reg, who used the van for his window-cleaning round, did not seem to appreciate the young Scouser's logic and asked him if he was 'taking the piss.' We left the kid bemused, standing by the now silent van, with his two bob bit still held high.

As we claimed a vantage point on the terraces, our travails were almost immediately rewarded in true West Ham fashion.

1963 – West Ham's third FA Youth Cup final: Charlo's final

The Anfield crowd were jubilant when, right at the start of the final, the home side scored an early goal. When a second went in on the stroke of the thirty-fifth minute, it looked like the start of a rout, but the red momentum was disturbed when John Dryden pulled one back for the Hammers. An injury to John Sissons, courtesy of Tommy Smith, who even then looked like Jack Palance in a particularly menacing role, reduced the West Ham striker's effectiveness in the second half. As the game went on, the young Irons started to flag badly and, regardless of the valiant defending of skipper Charles, Liverpool scored a third. This would have destroyed many teams, but despite the tender age of these boys from the Boleyn Ground, they pulled themselves up out of the mud in the final third of the game and dominated the field.

Following a move that started with a Charlo pass out of defence, Peter Bennett hit the post and wingers Dryden and Harry Redknapp had good chances cleared. In the end the scoreline did not really reflect the way the match had gone.

The second leg was held on a Saturday evening at Upton Park and I was one of the 13,200 Irons fans who turned out to cheer the youthful Irons.

West Ham were nervous at the start of the game. I am not sure that the enthusiasm of the crowd did much to help this, but they lost their inhibitions when Trevor Dawkins hit the net with a shot that flashed through a crowded penalty area.

However, the Irons had to continue to chase the game and it seemed the entire team were involved in constant up-field raids. John was banging in several threatening crosses. But Liverpool played the counter punch tactic well enough and hit the Hammers with 2 goals in three minutes to give them a 5-2 lead overall. The task now seemed hopeless, but Charles rallied his troops with the bluest of claret and blue language and, just before the break, Martin Britt headed West Ham back into the game. Within fifteen minutes of the second half, Britt got himself a second. It was 5-4, and for the first time we had the initiative.

Charlo was the complete captain. He had never given up. From where I was standing, close to the front of the North Bank (now the Centenary Stand), I could clearly see and hear his powerful commitment. Fists clenched, body bent slightly forward, he yelled at his team in ruggedly beautiful cockney tone, 'Cume oyn! We've fuckin' got 'em naa!' Harry Redknapp seemed inspired, but perhaps he was just terrified. Whatever the case, I was never to see him play better and it was his magnificent solo run that provided Britt with the ammunition to complete his hat-trick. There were three minutes on the clock and it seemed no-one in the crowd knew what would happen if the game ended in a draw. However, speculation became academic when Redknapp made yet another raid down the wing, finishing with the perfect cross for Britt to win the match for the home team.

The second game at Upton Park took place two days after the first leg. It seemed to take us about this time to get back to the East End. We had dawdled southward with Teutonic accompaniment all the way, turning many a head and inducing the odd straight-armed salute, sometimes with an Adolph impression thrown in for good measure. We broke down twice on the trek. On the first occasion, when the bonnet was opened, two pigeons flew out. The radiator was leaking, so Big Reg dug around in the back of the van and produced a half-empty packet of 'Scots Porridge Oats'. I was fascinated when he poured the contents into the radiator, adding water that he had begged for from a nearby house. But it worked and we continued our journey, chimes smashing on as if we were about to liberate the Fatherland. The engine boiled up again just beyond Birmingham. This time Reg produced two eggs from the glove compartment and cracked their yolks into the rad'. We took off again, and although I was half hoping that we would stop once more, just to see if Reg would chuck in a couple of rashers of bacon, we got home without further trouble. The most positive thing about the whole experience was that the power of a good breakfast had been truly fixed in my mind.

West Ham United, The FA Youth Cup winners, 6 July 1963. Harry Redknapp and Colin Mackleworth stand to the left of eighteen-year-old John, who will not let go of the trophy. Dennis Burnett is in the background. The shirtless Bill Kitchener and four-goal Martin Britt, who does the traditional hat thing, are on their skipper's right.

The young Hammers had achieved a fantastic victory. The Liverpool side that were beaten that Friday evening were to be the seed bed of the team that would dominate Europe for years later in the century. West Ham's captain that day had established himself as the hard man of the East End team, but Liverpool's own 'deterrent', the young Tommy Smith, the Anfield man of steel-to-be, was reduced to tears as John Charles led his team to collect the Cup. West Ham would not make the final again for a dozen years. John recalled:

> *I skippered the youth team because I was the most knowledgeable. I knew all the tricks of the trade didn't I. I was the pro'. They were all younger than me. I had the experience. Ron Greenwood made the decision. I will always remember the Youth Cup. It made history. I recall Greenwood saying to me, 'The next time I see you I want to see you up there holding the Cup'. He was so made up when we won. About 17,000 turned out at Upton Park that night, the Friday before the Cup final. Martin Britt was brilliant. He was in on everything. We came back to beat Liverpool. West Ham had lost the first leg at Anfield 3-1. Martin Britt had scored a vital goal though. Back at Upton Park we won 5-2, Britt scored three. Britty kept banging 'em in, heading 'em in. Harry Redknapp got a staff car that night.*

Ron Greenwood described the 5-2 win at Upton Park, which turned around a 1-3 defeat at Anfield, as 'wonderful'. Ten years of hard graft had brought the win that expunged the memory of two losses in the final.

The 1963 winners were young. Nine of the Youth side would still be available for the Youth Cup the following season. Only captain John Charles and Dennis Burnett would be too old. This was a team for the future. Apart from Charles and Britt, there was FA and Cup Winners Cup winner Johnny Sissons, and Division One players Dennis Burnett, Bill Kitchener, Trevor Dawkins (who also scored in the FA Youth Cup final), Bobby Howe, Peter Bennett and the West Ham manager-to-be Harry Redknapp. But John was the driving force and the heart of the side. Colin Mackleworth, the Hammers goalkeeper in that game, remembered, 'John looked after me and I roomed with him in Liverpool. At fifteen I was the baby of the team.'

Ten members of the Youth Cup winning side would go on to play for the senior side. Only Billy Dryden, a goal scorer, did not make it. In the 'other' FA Cup final of 1963, Sir Matt Busby's Manchester United beat Leicester City 3-1. David Herd got two goals and Denis Law also netted. The Beatles were number one in the charts with *From Me to You* and a pint of bitter cost 1s 5d.

'Players who manage to bring off the unexpected during a match should be encouraged.'

(*The Strategy of Soccer* – Johnny Byrne)

6

The Samurai Days

It is the way of the Samurai that even if one should suddenly have one's head cut off, one should still be able to perform one more action with certainty.
If one becomes like a vengeful ghost and shows great determination, even though one's head is cut off, one should not die.
Hagakure, The Book of the Samurai – Yamamoto Tsunetomo

As winter gave way to spring in 1963, John Charles was blossoming as a fine young footballer and the time came for him to move into the first team. Six victories had done a lot to ease the Hammers' relegation worries. They had pushed their way up to fourteenth place, but a home defeat to Everton and the loss away at Birmingham (both by the odd goal) was causing a late touch of the jitters at Upton Park. So in May, Greenwood decided to experiment with his defence in the home match against Blackburn Rovers. He brought the nineteen-year-old Charlo in to wear Bobby Moore's number six shirt. Bobby filled Ken Brown's number five slot. With John Lyall and Joe

John is at home in Ronald Avenue, Canning Town, 1963.

All the Hammers in the early sixties.

Kirkup making up the full-back pairing, West Ham looked to have put up a solid wall in front of the goalkeeper, Laurie Leslie. John recalled:

> *I think Ron gave some of us a go against Blackburn as a kinda reward for winning the FA Youth Cup. For a long time I was in what was known as the 'A' team. I made my debut in 1963 against Blackburn. That was also the first time John Sissons and Martin Britt played in the first team too. Ron Greenwood thought we deserved a try out. Blackburn won by the only goal of the game. I was playing against Ronnie Clayton that day, the England skipper. Keith Newton, the England defender, was also playing.*

John, alongside his defensive colleagues, did not have a bad game, but the forward line was ineffectual to the extent that Bobby Moore ended the game playing at centre-forward. For all that, Greenwood stuck with a lighter and overall more attack-orientated defence for the last three games, which included home matches against the two sides that would be relegated that term, Orient and Manchester City. West Ham finished off the season with a 6-1 win over City and managed twelfth place. Perhaps a more promising statistic was the season's goal count. It showed that the Hammers had scored more than they had conceded for the first time in years.

The whole world stopped on Friday 22 November 1963. President John Fitzgerald Kennedy was shot in Dallas, Texas. The shooting took place as the presidential motorcade drove through the city's main business centre. Three shots were fired from the sixth floor of a building. The President slumped forward, hit in the head and the neck. Kennedy died half an hour later.

Right: The England skipper, Ronnie Clayton, shakes hands with the Northern Ireland and Spurs captain, Danny Blanchflower, before the kick-off at Wembley. England won 2-1.

Below: Waiting for the future at 23 Ronald Avenue, E16.

West Ham's first major Cup trophy – the 1964 FA Cup. John Sisson (front left) holds the Cup with Geoff Hurst. Jack Burkett (left) looks on behind, with the winning goal scorer Ronnie Boyce (right), who, like John, was born in Ordnance Road, E16. In the background Eddie Bovington brings up the rear.

John Charles was to wait until February 1964 for his second senior game. It was the League Cup fourth-round tie away to Second Division Swindon Town. He came in to cover for Bobby Moore who was playing for England the next day. The 3-all draw meant a replay and John was part of the side that swamped the Robins 4-1 at Upton Park a couple of weeks after the match at the County Ground. However, Charlo did not play again in West Ham's first FA Cup-winning year. The Hammers were to be the last FA Cup winners to field only English players throughout the competition (see *The First and Last Englishmen*). Manchester City came very near to the feat in 1969 but played the Scot, Arthur Mann, brought to Maine Road from Hearts by former Hammer Malcolm Allison in November 1968, in their third-round win over Luton Town. West Ham also played an all English XI in the 1975 final but had called on Bermudan striker Clyde Best, who was to become a great friend of the Charles family. Coincidentally, he played in the fourth-round draw against Swindon Town, and again in the subsequent replay.

Although John missed out on the Cup campaign, it was not something he regretted. He told me, 'I was just happy to be playing and be part of it all. Of course I would have liked to have played, but it didn't really worry me.' The Cup taking up the focus at Upton Park meant that West Ham finished in fourteenth place in Division One. The side were back in the red in terms of League goals, but in a successful season in the FA and League Cups (the Irons reached the last four in the latter competition) they had netted 39 times, conceding only 18. So, overall, West Ham had amassed 108 goals and let in 92. Johnny Byrne was the club's leading scorer with 33 goals and deservedly won the 'Hammer of the Year' award. With Hurst's 26 goals, Budgie and Geoff were responsible for over half of the Hammer's goal tally.

In the 1964/65 term, West Ham's efforts were greatly concentrated on their campaign in the European Cup Winners Cup. Success in Europe was very dear to the heart of Ron Greenwood, who saw this as the true test of his footballing philosophy, which was based on sophisticated play and tactics and was built around the aesthetics of the game. The hard physical grind demanded in the English First Division and the requirement to fight out brutal battles on lower division grounds to attain cup success really did not suit Ron's taste.

As the Hammers marched on to European triumph, John was given just the single League outing. It was a late March fixture at Ewood Park, where Charlo played in the centre of the defence. Four days earlier, West Ham won the first and away leg of the European Cup Winners Cup quarter-final against Lausanne and, although Sealey and Scott hit the woodwork, Byron scored a hat-trick and the Irons were given a 4-0 drubbing. But good wins at home to Arsenal and at Villa Park set up an acceptable finish

West Ham's 1975 Cup-winning side, before the final against Fulham.

Front row: Harry Redknapp, Peter Brabrook, John Sissons, Jim Standen. JC, Dave Bickles, Jack Burkett, Ken Brown, Ron Boyce (getting off the bus), Martin Peters (on the bus), Johnny Byrne (driving), Alan Sealey (standing), in around 1965.

West Ham at the start of the 1965 season – The FA Cup, and having drawn with Liverpool, half the Charity Shield – most of the squad see the funny side.

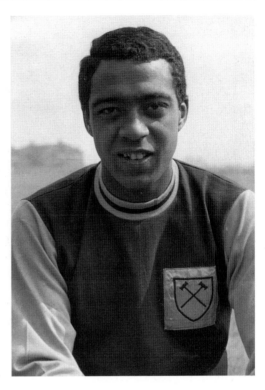

Hammers on the heart – 1965.

to the season and gave West Ham a respectable ninth position in Division One, which was an improvement of five places on the previous season, but the Irons only improved their points tally by two. However, victory at Wembley in the European Cup Winners Cup final, defeating TSV Munich 1860 2-0, was the crowning glory of the season and the Hammers' history at that point. As in the FA Cup, John was obliged to watch his eleven compatriot Englishmen and seven fellow East Enders become the first club to use only English players on the road to European glory. It is true that Tottenham were the first British team to win European silver in 1963, but they were truly a team drawn from the whole of the United Kingdom, with the Scot, Dave Mackay, moving mountains to get them to the final and their Irish skipper, Danny Blanchflower, being such a huge influence on the side.

It was in the 1965/66 season that John Charles began to make the West Ham number three shirt his own. He told me, 'When I switched to full-back that's when I played most of my games with Bobby' (Moore). Alongside England's captain, John would defend West Ham's honour for the rest of his football career. However, there were some players that would always cause trepidation in any defence. John told me:

There was one or two players I didn't like playing against, most of all George Best. I used to tell him to fuck off over the other side of the pitch – he'd just laugh. I used to always have a kick-up with Jimmy Robertson [Spurs and Arsenal] and Brian Douglas when we played Blackburn. Terry Paine, he played

John Lyall – West Ham to the core.

for Southampton, he was a hard player! I liked playing alongside John Lyall. Hard as nails John was. He was the type of bloke who helped yer. He was coaching from early on, even when he was playing. He would tell us, 'No-one's gonna pass us down this side today. They might get up the other side, but not this side'. When I played with John he was brilliant. He was better than Mooro! He used to play behind me and we used to just go out there, me and Johnny Lyall, and kick lumps out of 'em! 'They won't come past us', he used to say. He was a hard man yer know. He was a hard man.

According to his former West Ham Boys teammate, Charlie Green, 'John's best football was when he broke into the first team at West Ham.' Charlie made this statement with a strong certainty in his voice, 'His best football was that year and maybe six months the following year. After that first eighteen months, two years, I think he got a bit disheartened and it became just a job.'

Another comrade from John's days with West Ham Boys, Reg Leseurf, commented on John's application at the time. 'When he signed professional John wouldn't go in the café everyone else went in. It was more or less fries and fry-ups. That's all they did. The smell got on his clothes. He hated that. They used to give you the luncheon vouchers and he went along the Barking Road where you could get something healthier.'

Fields of iron

That season Charlo notched up 25 League appearances and was on the winning side on 10 occasions. However, perhaps one of his best performances was in a draw, when the Hammers visited Anfield early in the 1965/66 campaign. On an awful mid-September Wednesday evening, most of the 44,397 fans who turned out to see the champions expected to see at least a repeat of the 1-5 walloping that the Merseysiders had handed out to West Ham at Upton Park nine days earlier.

Anfield guerrillas

This was one of Liverpool's most fabulous sides made up of Lawrence, Lawler, Byrne, Milne, Ron Yeats, Stevenson, Ian Callaghan, Roger Hunt, Ian St John, Tommy Smith and the amazing wing wizard, Peter Thompson. The Irons had made a number of changes to the side that had been embarrassed at the Boleyn Ground. Dickie took Standen's place in goal whilst Bovington, Charlo, Peter Bennett, and Sissons replaced Bickles, Brabrook, Byrne and Scott in a line-up that also included Kirkup, Burkett, Moore, Peters, Hurst and Ron Boyce. West Ham gave a display of skill and courage which even the Kop fans were to applaud. It was a show of 'shut-em-out' brilliance that belied the previous 7-game sequence wherein the Hammers had conceded 15 goals.

Ronnie Clayton, Roy Vernon and
Bryan Douglas.

Martin Peters beats off a Liverpool/Roger Hunt attack. Jim Stanton attempts to cover and Bobby Moore looks on.

Charles took the centre-half role, linking defensively with the number-seven-shirted Bennett. Ticker Boyce played inside left. Unashamedly and probably correctly, the Hammers deployed often as many as nine men back in defence, seemingly camping in their own penalty area. At times it looked like the Hammers had circled the wagons, with Moore and Charlo foiling and thwarting, parrying and crushing at the centre. However, every now and then, the ball would be slipped through the blockade to Martin Peters, who would switch quickly between rearguard action and helping launch swift counter-attacks by the Irons' two-man attack force, Geoff Hurst and John Sissons. This interchange between trench warfare and guerrilla tactics paid off in the thirty-seventh minute. West Ham took the lead using the best of their ability to break from a defensive position and knock opponents back on their heels in shock.

Hurst, suddenly unmarked, was released by a Peters cross – the latter-day knight unleashed a 15-yard shot. Tommy Lawrence, the rotund Caledonian custodian of the Mersey-red nets, was, like an angelic boar, still hovering betwixt heaven and earth, stretching in defensive flight as the avenging comet tested the back of the mesh he guarded. From then on the onus was on Liverpool to take the game to West Ham. For those who had watched the Hammers' European Cup Winners Cup matches in Prague and Zaragoza the previous season, when the Irons had fought so tenaciously on foreign fields, these Lancastrian proceedings must have evoked highbred feelings

Bobby Moore leads West Ham out at Upton Park and Johnny Byrne follows.

somewhere between nostalgia and *déjà vu*. The battling Mooro of the first half became the majestic Bobby Moore, patron saint of English football in the second forty-five minutes, marshalling his ranks like the general he was, as the Scouse war-machine piled on the pressure. At the same time, Charlo grew to a colossus in the number five shirt, the fulcrum of West Ham's resistance, blocking wave after wave of crimson attrition.

In exasperation and desperation the miner, and son of a miner, Bill Shankly, sensing that his men were suffocating behind a claret-and-blue rock fall, withdrew his gladiatorial defender Chris Lawler and threw Liverpool's first ever League substitute, Geoff Strong, into the fray. Strong was sent in search of a chink of light in West Ham's wall of iron and in the seventy-sixth minute he felt air. The brave and, at points, inspired Alan Dickie was beaten by a glancing header from Anfield's initial twelfth man. The Kop drew breath – the relief was tangible. But there was no appetite for further adventure. Fearing another sucker punch, West Ham's version of Mohammad Ali's 'rope-a-dope', Liverpool gratefully settled for even honours.

Clash of the clarets

The following month saw the Hammers involved in another defensive battle at Turf Moor. For seventy-five minutes, West Ham staged a solid protective action against a ravaging Burnley side, who were to finish third in Division One at the end of the season, on equal points with the runners-up, Leeds, and just six points behind the champions, Liverpool. For most of the match it looked as if the East Enders would take a point home with them on the train back to the docklands. However, the clarets had a powerful forward line that included the Frankensteinesque Andy Lochead, back from two weeks in the purgatory of suspension and the anomalous, munchkin-like, straw-haired with a comb-over, ball-caressing genius, Ralph Coates.

In the last quarter of an hour, the team that Burnley chairman and potentate Bob 'I Claudius' Lord put together for £1,500 made the push that would nudge them in front of Leeds to take the top spot in Division One. Again, West Ham had looked a class act, being able to make threatening sorties up-field but holding onto the art of the organised retreat to form a solid wall across their 18 yard line and reversing the process to create sudden breakaways from defensive operations. But the Irons missed the cobra qualities of Johnny Byrne and Brian Dear when it came to making the most of the hit opportunities in this type of hit-and-run combat.

Defensively, Charles was outstanding, playing the elusive will-o'-the-wisp Willie Morgan brilliantly and Moore, in the best West Ham tradition, Cantwell and Bond-like, still found time to use the ball accurately. But apart from Charlo there was a tendency towards panic in the rest of the defence that had not been evident during the Anfield combat. Even the usually unflappable Bobby Moore fell into the trap at one point, making a suicidal back-pass early on, which should have presented Burnley with a goal start.

Despite his predominantly midfield role, Martin Peters was the top Hammers marksman during this game, twice going through alone to test the Burnley backstop Blacklaw with fast-rising volleys. Geoff Hurst worked hard enough to give him support, but both wingers were out of the game for long periods and Britt never showed the speed of thought to outwit the rugged Merrington.

When wiry Willie Irvine gave Burnley a thirty-seventh minute lead, grabbing the rebound after a fast cross-shot from Morgan had bounced off West Ham 'keeper Jim Standen's chest, the Irons responded swiftly. In arrears for no more than 200 seconds, the Hammers pushed forward. Martin Britt lost Merrington, his jailer for all but that instant, to head home a cross-of-fire from Burnett.

Willie Morgan in Manchester United incarnation is fighting off Alan Mullery of Spurs.

Sticking with their script, the Hammers produced another stunning retaliatory move in the sixty-fifth minute. Peter Brabrook and Geoff Hurst carved out a gem of a chance, but with only the 'keeper to beat, Hurst leant backwards and the ball zoomed over the bar. The miss was to prove the most costly of the game. It revived Burnley's fast-flagging confidence and just over ten minutes later they had netted again. Bandy Andy, ever handy, gratefully bedded a propitious rebound from an alarming clearance. Things then fell apart for the Hammers. With five minutes to go, Irvine, with his back to goal, turned in one gloriously flowing movement. It was one of those points where the idea that football is the working man's ballet makes complete sense; one of those soccer instances that seem to happen in slow motion, taking liberties with the moment, extracting the tocks out of time and extending the ticks to make them the harbingers

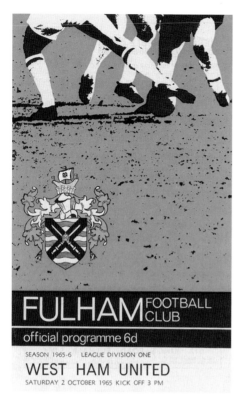

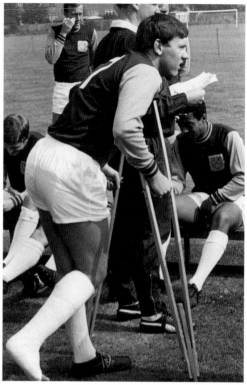

Left: Cottagers *v.* Hammers programme from 2 October 1965. West Ham lost, conceding three lucky goals.

Right: 'Wounded Stag' at West Ham Training Ground, Chadwell Heath. From left to right: Jack Burket (sitting), Joe Kirkup (standing), Brian Dear (with crutches and a broken ankle in the foreground). Behind him is Ron Greenwood, and behind him, Bobby Moore, and John Charles (sitting).

of glory or shattered hopes. Unfortunately for West Ham, in 1965, the day after firework night, which is always an anti-climatic time, the ball, maybe feeling particularly bouncy, danced a cheeky jig off Standen's chest then swung cheerily, making its merry way, seemingly waving to the crowd as it went, to nestle in the grass behind Jim's goal line. The smug little bastard!

Kleftica and chips

With their first game in their defence of the European Cup Winners Cup against Olympiakos Piraeus approaching, the fitness of West Ham's full-back pairing of the victorious Wembley team, Joe Kirkup and Jack Burkett, was uncertain. Both had been plagued by injury for most of the season and although they were playing reserve football in mid-November, Dennis Burnett and John Charles could rightly expect to get the nod for the game. Their 7-match first-team pairing had matured and started to prosper since they had come together in the Hammers' defence for the game against Fulham at the start of October 1965. Following the encounter with Burnley, Ron Greenwood had commented: 'Both boys played well. John was my Man of the Match. He was literally outstanding and had a great match. If he was six feet tall I'm certain he would be England's centre half. He is really tenacious. Dennis laid on the cross for our goal and has also been playing extremely well. If they continue to play like this it will take a great effort by any of our other full-backs to replace them. I shall not hesitate to play them against the Greeks if they show this form. They are young but the way we play our full-backs are not such key players as, say, the two men in the middle. Youngsters can do the job quite well.'

The latter part of this statement was typical of the kind of odd things Greenwood would say from time to time. The more he talked uninterrupted, the more he seemed to lose his way. In later years, after a traditional defeat in the early rounds of the FA Cup by a team from the lower reaches of the Football League, he finished a lengthy comment by saying, 'This is just not our type of competition.' Considering the Hammers' usual showing in League competition, it left one wondering exactly what he thought was West Ham's type of competition. He may have been thinking about being involved in Europe, but he might equally have thought that 'West Ham's type of competition' was 'one-and-in' or 'goalie rush!' Having apparently drew breath he went on, 'We are lucky to have so many full-backs playing well. In addition we have John Bond, Bill Kitchener, and youngsters like Frank Lampard and Bob Glozier. If nothing else, this is the something good that has come out of our present position.'

This might be seen to pass as Ron looking on the bright side. He certainly had a problem in terms of a strike partner for Geoff Hurst. The industrious number ten would score 40 goals by the end of all competitions, but his nearest rivals at the club were Martin Peters and Budgie Byrne with 17 each. Just before West Ham were due to play host to the Greeks, Byrne was nursing a foot injury. Greenwood's attacking options were further restricted due to Brian Dear's confinement to the 'A' team, needing to recover fitness levels after a long lay off, and the hero of the previous season's Wembley triumph, Alan Sealey, was walking with the aid of a stick. Ron Boyce, being limited to light training, would certainly not make the game.

For all this, Greenwood had some tricks up his sleeve. He had used a physical educationalist by the name of John Kane to give his players personality tests to examine 'the functional purpose of players'. Twenty of the first team were tested (the results were part of data used by Kane in lectures given during the Tokyo Olympics). That information must have had the Greeks quaking in trepidation and fear. Ron now knew that, for instance, the 'functional purpose' of his strikers was to make and score goals. All that he had to do now was find some to carry out their purpose.

Mighty Mariner minnows

Eleven days after the Turf Moor game and just a week before the Irons were due to open their second European campaign, John played in the quarter-final of the League Cup. West Ham had been taken to a replay in the second round by Bristol Rovers and had got past Mansfield and Rotherham for the honour of being entertained by Grimsby

Town. The Mariners had proved too much for Crystal Palace, Bolton and Preston, thanks in part to having the Football League's top scorer, Matt Tees, in their motley but committed ranks, not to mention the redoubtable Ron 'the doctor' Foster. Having seen West Ham's next League Cup opponents win at Selhurst Park, Greenwood commented as if Blundell Park had managed to attract the West German national side to the cause of Cleethorpes: 'They play fine football, calm and neat. They are an extremely good footballing side. They play a very useful 4-2-4 system and have had a lot of good results lately. It has taken them into second place in Division Three. It is not going to be easy for us. They have good players in Ron Foster, the former Orient forward and big scoring Matt Tees.'

It was Tees who put his side into the lead after eleven minutes. Charlo lobbed in what some saw as a freak goal to equalise after thirty-two minutes. It was his first and the penultimate goal for the first team. After Green put the home team ahead again 20 minutes into the second half, Geoff Hurst pulled the Irons level to earn the replay with a scrambled goal in the seventy-first minute. The Hammers went on to beat the giant killers at Upton Park by a single Hurst goal.

John kept his place for the first leg of the semi-final at Upton Park. Jimmy Scoular, the Cardiff manager, came with his team to the Boleyn Ground full of confidence, but goals from Bovington and Byrne in the first half and Brabrook and Sissons in the second seemed to put the tie beyond the Welsh side. However, a double strike from Andrews in the last 10 minutes gave the Bluebirds some hope, after the home side has missed innumerable chances, including Brabrook's failure to hit an open goal following a typically incisive and cutting pass from Martin Peters. But the Ninian Park men's heads went down again when Hurst hit a last-minute goal that came by way of a rather lucky bounce of the ball.

West Ham went on to defeat Cardiff 10-3 overall, but without the presence of John Charles in the second leg. He also missed West Ham's third consecutive Cup Final, the two-legged encounter against West Bromwich Albion. But despite beating the Baggies at Upton Park, the Hammers lost the League Cup Final on aggregate. With that defeat went the loss of the insurance of a place in Europe by way of the Fairs Cup. This was the last year the final of this competition was played on a 'home and away' format. In 1967 the trophy was decided at Wembley.

Aegean flames

Dennis Burnett was not chosen to start against Olympiakos, but the high point of John's season and maybe his career was his experience in West Ham's first game in their bid to hold on to the European Cup Winners Cup. The first leg was at Upton Park at the end of November. The defence looked solid with John in a full-back partnership with Joe Kirkup. Bobby Moore and Ken Brown made up the back four with Eddie Bovington linking with a mid-field line-up of Peter Brabrook, Martin Peters and Johnny Byrne supporting Geoff Hurst and John Sissons up front. The Irons came away 4-0 winners, but the Greeks had taken their toll, kicking and lashing out at any whiff of claret and blue, spitting and elbowing their way through the game. John Charles was the only new boy to European football in the West Ham XI. He was just twenty-one and looked a little

SOCCER STAR, September 29, 1967

SOCCER STAR

1/3

STEVE EARLE (FULHAM) and JOHN CHARLES (W. HAM)

So that is what happened to the World Cup ball! Charlo is about to give Steve Earle (Fulham) something to remember him by at Craven Cottage in 1967. Allan 'Sniffer' Clark (who would move on to Leeds and England fame) looks on in horror.

incredulous at times, aghast at the behavior of the Greeks, but he was able to give as good as he got and a few Olympiakos lads would remember the boy from Canning Town – one or two probably still carry the scars. He did well enough to keep his place for the second leg.

I was taken to the game by my cousin Bryan, who was a Petty Officer in the Navy at the time. We were accompanied by Bryan's boyhood mate from the manor, 'Laughing' Spam Fritter. I knew that could not possibly have been his name but everyone said it was his genuine handle and that is how he was known and referred to. I once asked him his real name and he told me 'Spamuel'. We arrived outside the stadium some hours before the game was due to kick-off and we were all ravenous, so we found a small café about fifteen minutes walk from the Olympiakos ground. We looked at the menu and saw that it was (how did we think this was unreasonable?) in Greek. Spam said 'leave it to me'. He called the waiter and pointing to himself and the two of us in turn, ordered, shouting in dulcet East End tones 'Taramasalata!' The waiter gave a double thumbs-up and, smiling with large yellowing teeth said, in a very thick accent but jaunty bon-vivant 'Awl ryte maties – Winnie Schtone Shurch Ill!' We returned the thumbs-up, or at least Bryan and I did. Spam gave what I hope our new Greek friend took to be a Churchillian victory sign. We waited just a few minutes for our trusty maître d' to return, and return he did as swift and as chirpy as a lark. Tray in hand, with a flourish he placed in front of us...three pints of lager.

It was indeed a European baptism of fire for young John Charles on his first trip to Europe in a serious senior football competition. West Ham literally got a firecracker of a welcome for the second leg in Greece. The 45,000 crowd were throwing them around the huge Olympiakos soccer bowl well before the match. They were lobbing them at the West Ham team as they inspected the pitch before the boys from Upton Park got changed. That was about an hour prior to the kick-off. A thunder-flash was burning away in Jim Standen's goal as he took up his place and the bombardment continued throughout the game.

Injuries meant that Martin Peters was moved to centre-forward. The side that took the field was Jim Standen, Joe Kirkup, John Charles, Eddie Bovington, Ken Brown, Bobby Moore, Peter Brabrook, Martin Peters, Johnny Byrne, Geoff Hurst and John Sissons. Both Standen and Hurst had been suffering with stomach bugs. This was part of the reason why Geoff played mostly a defensive role in the match. As the teams took the field, the hot afternoon was filled with a deafening chant of 'O-lym-pi-akos, O-lym-pi-akos' from the massed ranks of the Greek supporters. This created a strange contrast to the calm Aegean Sea in the background. The 126 claret and blue supporters did a good job in replying and the sound of *I'm Forever Blowing Bubbles* drifted over the landscape like a light sea mist. *'I've Got a Lovely Bunch of Coconuts'* hit the air a little harder.

From the off it was clear that the Greeks were going to continue with their rough and uncompromising style. The Greek World Cup skipper, Polychoronu, was quick to make his mark and he chose to make it on Martin Peters, giving him a nasty gash on his shin that looked the better part of a foot long, after just twenty minutes. Peters had gone down but only for a few seconds and, though most fans would not know it, his fellow professionals in England knew him to be a hard player. Whilst he was down though, Polychoronu allowed himself a smirk towards his teammates. However, the smile left his face as he sensed a cold stare grinding into him. He caught John Charles' emotionless gaze and for a moment froze. He knew instinctively that he was now a marked man. In the Easterly maze of life where John Charles and Martin Peters were born, you looked after your own. It was just a matter of time now. Vengeance may well be the Lord's but Polychoronu was Charlo's; the hunter had become the hunted.

The Hammers had a couple of first half shots. One, from Martin Peters, was particularly unlucky, being just inches wide, but the first goal was a bit fortunate. Stefanakos missed a chip forward by Sissons, and Peters scored with an angled shot that was deflected past Fronimidis by a defender. Peters was to say later that he had meant it to go to Johnny Byrne. As the teams went in at half time, it was clear that West Ham were not doing too well. Too many passes out of defence were going astray.

West Ham's second goal was an Irons special. It was just a few minutes after the kick-off for the second half that Byrne sent John Sissons away. The Middlesex boy jinked around a couple of defenders and flighted a perfect cross to the head of Maestro Martin Peters. As with his first goal, Peters' effort was greeted by the Greek crowd with almost perfect silence. The West Ham supporters, of course, went mad and for a few moments the strains of *Knees Up Muvver Brown* echoed around the hushed Hellenic arena.

Eddie Bovington scored a strange own goal just three minutes later, sending a lofty ball past the unbelieving Standen. At this, the Piraeus crowd erupted into an eye-bolting, arm-waving, jumping-up-and-down, screeching mass. This reaction was doubled when Polychoronu converted a penalty. Ken Brown was picked out as the offender by the Russian referee, Bahramov. The decision was a complete mystery. Even the usually sedate Greenwood questioned the Soviet official (Geoff Hurst would meet this man again in the incarnation of the linesman who helped him make history in the summer of 1966). But it was too little too late as far as the Greeks were concerned and West Ham's home-leg margin of victory never looked threatened, unlike Polychoronu.

Late in the match the Greek skipper gathered the ball close to West Ham's left touchline. Polychoronu saw Charlo coming in from a long way off. John had started his run from 30 yards. But the prey was helpless. There was nothing he could do but wait; the fates had spoken. John hit his target like the last tram out of Custom House on New Year's Eve. The Greek flew high and long – he would have had enough time in the sky to catch a glimpse of the faces in the crowd, wincing in expectation of the coming damage. The sickening thud with which he hit the ground was only rivalled by the cavernous crash John had made on impact. As play continued and Polychoronu lay motionless, the Olympiakos defender Pavlidis, as if his mind were made up to settle scores, made for John. However, he seemed to quickly reassess matters as the boy from E16 turned to face him.

Somehow Polychoronu staggered upright as the final whistle of the tie blew, but that was not the end of the epic. It continues in the form of legend, as there are those on the shores of the Aegean who still tell of the dark and handsome boy from the West with eyes of fire and a soul of flame.

After the match Greenwood identified Standen as Man of the Match, pointing out the magnificence of two saves in the first part of the game. He said that Jim had been outstanding. Ron also praised the rest of the lads for facing up to the more than intimidating crowd, but Martin Peters was the hobbling hero.

The West Ham side, with John amongst them, boarded their plane home, which was a British Eagle Britannia bearing the name *Justice*. Justice is something you give, but like power, it also needs to be taken, and the brave Hammers had made sure justice had been done.

Borussia Balls-up

John missed the quarter-final games against Magdeburg – Burnett and Jack Burkett were the full-back pairing for both legs of that tie – but he played in both semi-final matches against Borussia Dortmund. West Ham were beaten in both games, whilst Greenwood was arguing with his skipper, Bobby Moore, about wages – a few pounds. The captaincy was given to Johnny Byrne, a great individual player and, unlike Bobby, a talker on the park (hence his nickname 'Budgie') but not an experienced captain at top level. Moore was no ordinary skipper. The debates that err toward the role of captain being irrelevant or merely symbolic cannot be applied to him or his professional context in the sixties. After Malcolm Allison left Upton Park in the 1950s (the man who mentored the young Moore) and Noel Cantwell had, a little later, moved to Manchester United, (these were the players who had run training sessions for youngsters on Tuesdays and Thursdays and led the tactical discussions that had become part of club life at Upton Park), Bobby took over as the informal leader of the club's professionals. It was he who interpreted and built on Greenwood's ideas on the field and he that made any strategy work – West Ham played around Bobby Moore. The cost of Greenwood's and/or the club's meanness and the bickering that resulted from the same thing must have been huge to West Ham and was to have lasting effects. Borussia went on to beat Liverpool in the European Cup Winners Cup final at Hamden Park after extra time. West Ham had matched Liverpool in the Charity Shield at the start of the 1965/66 season and at Anfield in the League. Both Liverpool and Dortmund went on to become veterans of European competition and this allowed Liverpool to build the foundations on which they were to become one of the world's super clubs by the last part of the twentieth century. Who knows what would have happened to the Hammers, including the budding England Youth defender John Charles, if they had been led into those semi-final games by the only captain most of them had known as professional footballers, the greatest ever England skipper, the man who would inspire his country to win the World Cup just a few weeks later? What would have been the effect on John Charles' chances of being selected for the England World Cup squad if he had been part of a successful European trophy winning side just weeks before the biggest sporting tournament ever to be held within British shores?

Johnnie for England!

West Ham, as usual, lacked consistency over the season and finished in twelfth spot in Division One. As the Irons' schedule came to an end, John was not too far from getting full international recognition. His wife Carol recalled: 'Alf Ramsey phoned up for him and I said he was over the road mending his mate's car. Alf asked me to get hold of him as he wanted him to play that night. John was drinking in the Greengate [a Barkingside hostelry]. I ran round to the pub and told John he had to come home.

> *I was in the Greengate having a glass of ale and was told to report that evening. It was one of those out-of-season games, like England A v. England B, England against 'The Rest'. That game used to be before the FA Cup final. We had to meet at Lancaster Gate. It was at Highbury and I played for 'The Rest' that night. Mike Summerbee was in the side. I must have done alright because I went with*

Left: Narnas, one an' a tanna. *Right:* Bobby Moore – no ordinary skipper.

England to Jersey and played a Jersey XI. Jimmy Greenoff [the marvellous Leeds player] was playing. It was like an Under-23 game. I liked Alf Ramsey, he was very quiet, but a good manager. A very nice bloke and made you feel welcome.

Then John showed just a hint of a lack of self confidence, 'I wasn't good enough to play for England. I was just ordinary. I wasn't tricky, I wasn't fancy. Cohen and Wilson had played a hell of a lot of games for their clubs. I had made the Youth team and that was it really.' As someone who watched John play I could not agree with this. I could not help but understand this summation of his own abilities as an expression of John's modesty. Neither Cohen or Wilson were 'fancy' – they and John were very much in the same mould as Alf when he was a player at Spurs. It may be that John was much closer to full international recognition than he allowed himself to believe.

Unfortunately most reflections on the football career of John Charles portray him as a workman-like player. Phrases like 'tough' and 'reliable' abound. John was an unpresumptuous man and, like many East Enders of his generation, not prone to purple phrases or self-praise. This being the case, he tended to agree with this type of assessment of his qualities. However, although never given to boasting in any serious way, he did, from time to time, demonstrate that he had much more talent than the traditional

Alf Ramsey, the England manager, asks three squad members, including former Hammer John Smith and Iron-to-be Jimmy Greaves, 'Who you looking at?'

analysis of his capabilities might suggest. His youngest son, Mitchell (also known by family and friends as Mitch or Butch) told me of the kind of finesse he was capable of: 'It was down the fruit and veg market, Spitalfields, a few years ago, I couldn't believe it! I was fifteen or sixteen. There was a salesman, maybe two years older than me. He says, "I hear you used to play football, Charlo. Was you any good?" Dad says, "Yeah, I was alright." So this bloke says, "Well how good was yer?" And Dad said, "Well can you do this?" He put his hand in his pocket, pulled out a tenpence piece and he flicked it up in the air. He caught it on his toe, on his shoe, kicked it back up high over his head, opened his jacket and it went straight in his inside pocket. I've only ever seen him do something like that about twice in me life!'

John's game was based on a type of warrior logic – a kind of pragmatism that brushed everything else aside. There is a Samurai saying that states that one should '…take an enemy on the battlefield as a hawk takes a bird. Even though the hawk may be in the midst of a thousand birds, it will pay no attention to any other than the one it has first marked.'

That was the kind of focus John had. He told me, 'Me, I wanted to win! Any old how. Nothing to do with the "West Ham way".' Charlo would not be deflected from his task, which was to stop opposing players scoring or making a chance to score. He told me, 'I never had any rituals or lucky charms.' He laughed at the idea.

Although a fine controller of the ball, John was, in every sense, a defender in the gladiatorial mould. He was sometimes obliged to take as good as he got, but this never dampened his good humour or ability not to take himself too seriously. In his autobiography, *Bonzo* (1988), Billy Bonds, no shrinking violet himself, recalls John commenting after a bruising game at Port Vale, 'They've left me white and blue all over!'

John Charles was a solid, physical player, but he was able to attack down the flanks in a way that would not become widely used until twenty years after he left the game. He was a wingback before wingbacks existed, although he was anything but a prolific scorer. He ran out for the Hammers 35 times during the 1966/67 term and it was during this campaign that he scored his first and last League goal. With a distinct sense of amused irony he told me:

> *I got two goals for the first team. The first was against Grimsby in the League Cup and the other against Manchester United, when they won the League in '67. They beat us 1-6. Martin Peters reckoned he touched it before it went in, but he got plenty, it didn't hurt him to let me have one.*

Charlo Law-breaker

I was at Upton Park that day, standing squeezed in the old North Bank. As the crowd left after the game I recall just lifting up my legs and being carried out by the crush. That day stuck in the memories of many supporters. One who I came across during the writing of this book remembered: '…the infamous game against Man Utd. As good as West Ham were at that time, unfortunately there was nothing they could do about a superb performance by Best, Law, Charlton and company. In fact Charles had a torrid time against the formidable Law, who not only beat players by his skill – he also taunted them all the time. Poor Charles, I remember (because this was one of those outstanding games that will always stay with you) was duped into giving away a penalty by reacting with a push on Law to a sly slap around the face. This, coupled with the atmosphere and the throwing of flour bombs (and the result), ended with crowd violence erupting in the North Bank… Later in the match Charles had another altercation with Law (who was really verbally assaulting Charles) which made him dive in. Being in the Chicken Run at the front I can tell you it got really ugly, and from what I remember Law played the rest of the game in the centre of the pitch.'

Spurs spannered

I had also been at White Hart Lane some months earlier, along with over 57,000 others, and I think I saw one of the finest games John played for West Ham. Afterwards the match was called 'the best match of the year' in the press, even though England had just won the World Cup. The week before, West Ham had beaten Fulham 6-1 at the Boleyn Ground, so they made their way to White Hart Lane with the confidence that they might inflict defeat on those Spurs of North London in their own cockerel's roost.

Jimmy Greaves hit the bar in the first minute and scored from a penalty after being slain, laid low and nailed by Eddie the Bov. Dagenham lad Jimbo missed his second spot kick of the game (the first one he had failed to put away as a Tottenham player) after Bobby Moore had handled the ball. Charlo seemed to be involved in everything except goalkeeping and covering the ball boys. He worked up and down the pitch seemingly tirelessly, constantly animated and up for the fight. In all, Spurs struck post and bar three times – woefully unlucky, but, undeniably wonderful in a 'I love to see Spurs get beat, especially by West Ham' sort of way. Johnny Byrne, Peter Brabrook, John Sissons and Geoff Hurst scored for the Hammers with Terry Venebles and Alan Gilzean adding to Jimmy G's pen.

Ah! Alan Gilzean! Those were the days when kids could run up to players on the pitch and ask for an autograph as they warmed up. I was never an autograph hunter and certainly would not ordinarily have contemplated asking any non-West Ham player for their signature. However, the kid who I went to the match with, a fat lad called Batson (Batty Fatson as he was curiously known) wanted the dour Scot's moniker for his collection and persuaded me to beg for it. I trotted up to the balding goal-line bandit like some soapy git from *The Famous Five* and chirped, 'Can I have your autograph Mr Gilzean?', offering Fatson's pristine book and parker pen. 'Will ye nay fook off?' he responded with all the eloquence of the Burns tradition. I stood smiling stupidly for a moment as he trotted away (Gilzean never 'ran' anywhere – trot was his top gear). As he moved off he thoughtlessly spat in my direction. I have never felt this was malicious as it was done in a very informal, unselfconscious, devil-may-care manner, but the liberal gob landed smack on Fatson's book, placing a kind of opaque seal over the name of Alan Mullery. I returned, Mercury like, to Fatson with the clear evidence of my rebuttal. He wept bitterly for most of the match as the flob refused to dry and allow him to pick off the resulting carapace, so saving Mullers and lowering the risk of pages (together with Gilzean and Mullery...ugh!) being forever bonded together. For years later I never spat, gobbed or flobbed...I 'Gilzeaned'.

At that time the Four Tops were number one with *Reach Out I'll be There* and, at Hartlepool, the thirty-one-year-old Brian Clough was. He decided to work for nothing until the club sorted out its finances. Brian Clough? Finances?

Mile End to Nile Bend

That Spurs game was one demonstration of John's tremendous innate stamina and genuine turn of speed. He was a natural athlete and, alongside the boys he grew up with in football, Martin Peters and Bobby Moore, he was able to read the game far better than many of his defensive contemporaries. Just a few weeks after the game against Tottenham, West Ham made the then fifteen-hour journey to Cairo to take on the Egyptian national team (which is unthinkable as a mid-season prospect today). Let no-one mistake, at this point in his early twenties John Charles was England quality. He played as well as any full-back I have seen in that match, alongside the exquisite Mooro, exhibiting a cultured understanding of the game as well as a rock-like presence in defence. Had Alf Ramsey seen that match, and had he not valued experience so highly, the back four of the England World Cup side might well have been stiffened by John Charles of West Ham United.

Another consideration that went against John's selection for England was that West Ham was not a defence-minded team. Greenwood did not believe that one should build on defence, the prevailing philosophy of some of the leading clubs of the time; Ron looked to create a kind of 'balance', of the sort the great Dutch sides achieved in their 'total football' era, a sort of harmony across the team. This produced exciting football and, at times, an aesthetic that bordered on art. It generated movement that transcended sporting excellence and entered the realms of poetic beauty, but it was not the most effective means of achieving results in the mêlée that was Division One in the mid-sixties. In 1966/67 West Ham again finished in the bottom half of the table (sixteenth). The team conceded 84 goals and scored 80. The champions, Manchester United, scored just four more goals than the Hammers, but they let in only 45.

For the Samurai there is something to be learnt from a rainstorm. When meeting a sudden shower, you will try not to get wet and run quickly along the road. By doing such things as passing under the eaves of houses you will still get wet.

When you resolve this from the beginning you will not be perplexed when you still get the same soaking.

This understanding extends to all.

Hagakure, The Book of the Samurai – Yamamoto Tsunetomo

7

American Dream,
Real Madrid, Final Bow

In the words of the ancients, one should make one's decisions in the space of seven breaths – this is a matter of being determined to break right through to the other side. So, when one makes a decision to kill, even if it will be very difficult to succeed by advancing straight ahead, it will not do to think about going about it in a long, roundabout way. The way of the Samurai is immediacy. It is best to dash in headlong.

Hagakure, The Book of the Samurai – Yamamoto Tsunetomo

A while before the 1-6 débâcle at the hands of United, West Ham had undertaken an end-of-season odyssey. After departing from Heathrow on Sunday 16 April, between two depressing home defeats by Yorkshire clubs Sheffield United and Leeds, the Tyke-torn Hammers took the eighteen-hour flight to Houston, Texas.

My nautical cousin Bryan again sorted everything out for me to get to the game. It was just him and me this time. Laughing Spam Fritter was paying his debt to society after being caught diamond smuggling. He went hobbling past Dover customs one day as if he was walking on hot coals. The rocks he had stashed in the turn-downs of his socks had somehow, from ship to shore, made their way to the souls of his feet just at the wrong time. It was something of a relief when he heard the call 'Oi you! Hop along'. Re-christened, 'Ice-Feet Spam', he was ensconced at Her Majesty's Good Nick, Pentonville, presumably laughing on the other side of his big old spam face.

We flew out from Brise Norton in what I took to be a cargo plane. It was a journey to rank with my Youth Cup final trip to Liverpool, only the suffering was more protracted. Looking back, it was worth it.

On their arrival in America, the West Ham party were taken to a grand reception and undertook 'live' interviews on radio and television. Several players made personal appearances in the cause of promoting 'soccer' on 'the other side of the pond'. On the following Wednesday the Hammers ran out in the mighty Astrodome, a stadium light-years ahead of anything that existed in Europe at the time, to face the legendary Spanish giants, Real Madrid, led by their international skipper Francisco Gento. Also in the Real XI were the World Cup stars Pirri Zoco and Amaro Amacio. Over 33,000 cheered the teams onto the pitch, which was a huge crowd by American soccer standards of the time.

The wondrous cross

Madrid got off to a perfect start. After just five minutes Jim Standen punched a cross straight to Felix Ruiz, who sent in a shot that was deflected into the net. But before a minute had elapsed the Irons equalised. A claret and blue defender had blasted out of defence, skipping a tackle and ploughing directly through another. He covered almost the length of the field before he turned to cross the ball. He looked up for something much less than a second and let loose at his target – the head of Geoff Hurst. The connection went past Antonio Betancour from all of 12 yards.

The cross that had been converted into the header would have had to come in like a bullet, straight and true, with the minimum of spin, although what rotation there was would have to have been in an anti-clockwise direction, given the position of Hurst in relation to the goal. The altitude of the ball needed to be perfect. If Geoff had been obliged to jump to reach the ball he would not have had the strength of purchase that is possible driving through the ball from a firm base, with feet on the ground. The cross had to have been hit exceedingly hard because when the ball struck Hurst's forehead it would have immediately lost maybe as much as sixty per cent of its velocity, however as the Hammer forward changed the ball's trajectory it had to have maintained enough power to carry for a dozen yards and to have held enough speed to thwart the 'keeper.

Only one man on the field that day could have hit a ball like that. He watched the goal fly in from a point way out on the wing as he had done so many times before at Cumberland Road, on the Memorial Grounds, at Upton Park and all over England. The cheers rang out, but the cross, as it had pelted in, had whispered 'Charlo'.

Ramon Grosso, the Spanish centre-forward, began to combine dangerously with Amacio, troubling the Hammers defence almost constantly, but it was José Veloso who smashed a low shot home with just nine minutes on the clock. The game was on fire now and the crowd were on their feet, energised by the non-stop cut and thrust. The adrenaline was seemingly transferring from the spectators as the players abandoned prudence, allowing inspiration to take over. This was now more than an interesting encounter. This was a confrontation, a duel of football cultures. Two sides, of no mean cities, were now locked in the embrace of sporting combat.

As the game moved through its falls and eddies, it became clear that the Madrid sweeper system was blunting West Ham's attacking potential. After half time this was the base that allowed Real to continue their offensive onslaught almost untroubled, the Hammers being effectively compartmentalised, the links between defence, midfield and attack having been as good as severed. It was not long before Amacio gathered a pass from Pirri and danced his dance of death through the Iron's lines to put his side further ahead.

Just when it looked as if the well-travelled East Londoners would succumb, Johnny Sissons, who was to be voted 'player-of-the-night' by the Houston crowd and media presenters, dragged his team back into the fight. The move started with Moore robbing Amacio with a delicate tackle that with Artful Dodger-like graft just pinched the ball from the Spaniard. The West Ham skipper could not pass the ball forward as was his wont as Pirri had blocked his angle, so instead he slid the ball to Charles. John had moved beyond Pirri to his left and had made up his mind what he was going to do with the ball before he had even made his run. He sent the ball right across field to Peter Bennett, who himself had rushed out of defence. Bennett now had the time to measure and make an inch-perfect pass to Sissons, who was able to simply side-foot the ball home. There was just over twenty minutes of the match left.

By now the spectators in the Astrodome were split. Many were cheering on the limey underdogs, but the appreciable Mexican population of Houston had a decent representation in the crowd and they were throwing their weight behind their Spanish cousins. This, together with the breathless competition at field level, created a powerful, intoxicating, almost overpowering atmosphere. Caution had been strangled by commitment and all life, all meaning, seemed to be concentrated in the game, the match, the contest.

It was all down to will in the last moments and it looked like Real were becoming overwhelmed, their essence simply worn down by the exuberant endurance of their opponents. They began to back off and protect their slender lead like a precious, vulnerable child. A display of negative football in the dying minutes of the game denied West Ham a deserved draw.

After the match Ron Greenwood said that, 'The Spaniards played fantastic stuff against us in the first half and we responded. This was one of the greatest games we have played in a very long time.' The American media seemed equally impressed, seeing the match as the perfect appetiser for the new twelve-team United Soccer League that would include the 'Houston Stars'. It was so typical of West Ham to be able to match the likes of Real Madrid just a few weeks after being humbled 3-1 by Second-Division Swindon, having been forced to replay a third round FA Cup tie following an embarrassing 3-3 result in front of over 37,000 of their own fans. Some things never change!

Back to the future

West Ham called on John just nineteen times during their Division One 1967/68 trials. He did play in all three of the Iron's League Cup matches. Another 'average' performance in Division One placed the Hammers in twelfth spot. However, the following season John made 35 League appearances, helping his side back into the top half of the table (eighth).

It seemed that the future was bright for the good-looking lad from Canning Town. Certainly the next decade would be full of incident for him, his team and those he loved, but whilst John was at Upton Park, the club and family were always connected. John recalled: 'I was in the Olympic Hotel San Francisco when I got notification of the birth of our first daughter.'

THE OLYMPIC

HCA AND WESTERN HOTELS
ONE WORLD OF FINE HOTELS

A TELEPHONE MESSAGE FOR...

MR JOHN CHARLES
ARRIVE 5-8-69

DAUGHTER BORN 430 A M THURS
WEIGHT 8 LBS 2 0Z
ALL IS WELL
LOVE CAROL & KEITH

MAY 8   TS 1250 PM   44

MC

Hello Lesley!

The Newham Recorder of Thursday, 15 May 1969, reported: 'A chance 6.30 transatlantic phone call on Thursday morning from West Ham United full-back John Charles, brought for him the news that he had become the father of a daughter – just two hours earlier! Lesley Charles weighed in at 8lb 2oz. John and Carol already have a son, Keith (3).'

Carol added: 'I'd just had my Lesley and he's gone to America. He went on the Monday; I was due to have my baby on the day that he went! I had her at half-past four and he was the first one to know.'

John was involved in what had become a tradition under Ron Greenwood, a post-season American tour, playing against Wolves, Aston Villa, Kilmarnock and Dundee United. These teams played each other twice in Kansas, Atlanta, Baltimore, St Louis and Dallas. The Irons also fitted in the odd friendly against the likes of Spurs. This kind of thing, of course, would seem unthinkable now, given the worries about players being involved in too many games. Clyde Best, who was then a teenager, signed professional forms for West Ham just before the Hammers departed for the US. He did well in his first game, scoring against Wolves.

But what seemed like being the zenith of John's career quickly turned into its downfall. What turned out to be a plague of injuries started in the autumn of 1969 and limited him to just five games up to the start of spring 1970. However, this did not stop John making a little bit of history. On 2 April that year he ran out at Upton Park with his great friend Clyde Best, the big Bermudan international who John and his family had 'adopted', taking him into the their home when he arrived in Britain to play for West Ham. It was the first

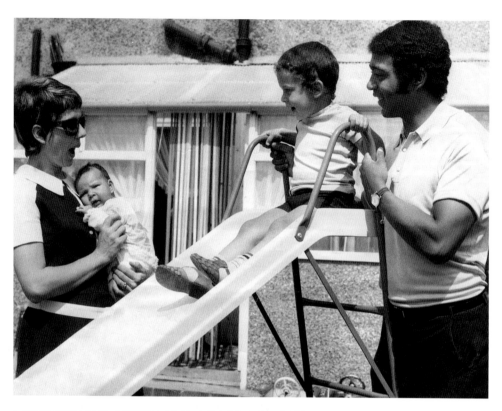

Above: And then there were four – John, Keith and in Carol's arms, Lesley.

Left: Clyde Best plays it cool, while Upton Park's west stand looks on.

time that two black Hammers had played together at the Boleyn Ground. Clyde grabbed the opening goal in a 2-2 draw with Leeds United, who would finish runners-up to Everton in the Division One Championship that season. It was a good performance for a side that would finish fifteen places behind the Peacocks. Almost poetically and certainly tragically, this was the last match John would play in the top flight.

John left West Ham in the summer of 1971. He was only twenty-six. He turned down a chance to join Orient, which was then managed by former Hammer Jimmy Bloomfield. He told me,

> *I kept getting this hamstring problem. In those days they couldn't mend 'em like they do with Lynford Christie, so he's back for a race the next day. You used to be out for two or three months. Every time I was training and I stretched it a bit it went. They took me up to a big hospital up town and the consultant said that the scar tissue kept on breaking down. I don't know if they wanted to operate on me or what, they said it might get better. In the meantime Carol's dad had the market stalls, he was a greengrocer.*

By this time John had two children to support, Keith, who had been born on 12 May 1966 and Lesley, who came into the world on 8 May 1969. There was also a third on the way (who would be called Mitchell, and who arrived on 10 October 1971). So the decision to give up football was also influenced by financial considerations; 'At West Ham I was earning £65 a week. My first week as a barrow boy I got £200. I started with Carol's dad, Ernie Gingell. Once I got into it that lark I really loved it. I became me own gov'nor and met different people. It was nice.'

But John kept up contact with his former associates in the game. His eldest son Keith particularly remembered the Boxing Day parties, 'For years and years they happened. It was often after the West Ham/Tottenham games. The two teams used to come back. I was just three or four and I'd be at the top of the stairs and listen to the dancing and talk downstairs.'

John had spent most of his career playing under Ron Greenwood and he was quite clear about his relationship with his manager:

> *Greenwood was a bit careful, maybe sly even. For instance, he'd just leave you out and not tell you. I hardly ever spoke to him as it happens, no-one did really. People did have a go at Greenwood every now and then. I think him and Bobby had their rows. What they was about I don't know. I think he said something to Harry [Redknapp] once and Harry got annoyed and slung a cup at him. I think it shattered against a wall. He was angry but again I don't know what it was all about.*
>
> *I was never one of Ron's boys. John Sissons was, but everyone else in the club hated him.* [John guffawed.] *Me and Eddie Bovington got a photograph out the other week; this was round Eddie's house. I pointed to John Sissons and I said, 'What words did you ever say to that feller while he was at the club Ed?' And he said, 'Fuck all'.* [John laughed hard. But he was quickly serious.] *I think a good*

Carol with her and John's first-born, Keith.

*manager gets to know the boys who've they've got. He'll mix with 'em. The more
you mix with 'em the more you know.*

For all this, Greenwood recognised John's gifts. He once described him as, 'A prince of
a player, he was a good, strong, straightforward competitor whose influence was significant.' At the same time John was quite aware of his manager's qualities,

*Greenwood was a good coach, knew what he was talking about. I was a good
defender, good at winning the ball. I got it and passed it and when Ron brought
in the idea of overlapping, I could do that well, I got in a few good crosses. I
remember Greenwood showed us one game on a projector – it had no sound,
it might have been our 8-0 win against Sunderland in '68. I think that was my
best game. I remember Peter Brabrook saying, 'Chas, you had it off there!' Ron
was a great coach, he knew the game. He decided how we would play. He'd say
to me, for instance if I was playing against say any quick wingers, I thought this
was good, you know, 'When wingers come up to a full-back they wanna go past
yer on the outside don't they, they wanna go by yer'. So he got me, if the winger
was trying to go by me, make 'em come across field. So you jockied them across
field so they was doing no damage. When they was half way across that's when
you kicked them up in the fucking air.* [John roared with amusement.]

Rokermen rocked

The Sunderland game of 19 October 1968 was a record equalling win for the Hammers. The Rokermen arrived at Upton Park, tenth place in the Division One table, having been defeated just 4 times in their 14 League games. West Ham were 4 places above the visitors but had failed to win a match in 7 previous attempts.

The Hammers had almost taken the lead via Harry Redknapp in the first seconds of the game. Jim Montgomery, the fine Sunderland 'keeper, was troubled thrice more by West Ham shots, each one a near thing. Just before the game had been going twenty minutes, Martin Peters floated in a cross that Hurst converted, diving full-length and driving the ball into the net with his fist. It was a clear handball to anyone standing behind the goal, but the referee Burns signalled a score. To his credit, after the game Hurst did admit to cheating.

Five minutes later, West Ham were awarded a free-kick after Eire international Charlie Hurley had been penalised. As was the norm Bobby Moore took it – what was unusual was that he scored. He hit a 35-yarder with the outside of his right boot which gave Montgomery no chance. As play was restarted it was clear that the Irons had smelt blood. Brooking and Bonds worked together to create a far-post chance for Hurst to head home. It was still ten minutes from half time and West Ham were 3-0 up.

Sunderland seemed to have managed to get to the break without further damage but within the dying seconds before the whistle, Billy Bonds' short corner was picked up

John Charles, 1968. John said that he liked to play against 'Anyone, so long as it's a League or Cup game. I hate friendlies.'

by Redknapp, who hit the ball into the centre and there was Hurst to volley it hard into the net. That was Geoff's first hat-trick in a year of trying.

Sunderland had nowhere to go as the second half started and they were beginning to become confused. As such, Sissons, Brooking and Peters found it easy to collaborate in providing the ammunition for Hurst to start on his second hat-trick of the afternoon. Geoff killed the ball with his chest and hammered it beyond poor Montgomery, who even the most ardent West Ham supporter was now beginning to pity. He had not had a bad game, but the Irons had overrun his defence and, for the most part it was him against a deluge of claret and blue. The sixth goal was again Hurst's. He picked up a stray rebound at 25 yards and hit it with force and without mercy. Montgomery grabbed at the thinnest of thin air.

Sunderland's defence was now helpless. If their morale had not already completely dissipated, it did when they allowed Brooking the chance to fire in a scoring shot. Less than a minute later, a terrible pass from Herd was picked up by Brooking, who sent Redknapp on a run down the right. As the carrot-topped wing man reached the end of his journey, he delivered a shallow cross to Hurst who, almost inevitably, completed his double hat-trick. This equalled West Ham's individual scoring record for a League game, set by Vic Watson in the 8-2 defeat of Leeds United in February 1929 and beat Brian 'five-goal-in-one-game'. This was Dear's post-war scoring record. It was a shame that such a landmark game was watched by West Ham's smallest home gate of the term – 24,718.

A certain hack had it that 'West Ham played no better than when I saw them draw at Tottenham and Sheffield Wednesday. There is genius in their play, but they are balanced on such a knife's edge that they can as easily fall one way as the other. Yesterday they fell the right way.'

However, *The Observer* was more generous when it reported: 'Hurst was allowed to keep the match ball, which was only proper since he had it for most of the afternoon.'

What most commentators missed was the performance of the West Ham defence that day. Bonds, Charles, Stephenson and Moore had isolated Mulhall, Suggett, Brand and Harris and condensed the play to the last third of the field at times. The Hammers guard was so dominant that Bonds and Moore were able to reinforce the attack for much of the game, leaving Charles and Stephenson to ward off the entire Sunderland response. This is what gave Hurst such fine service and why John saw this encounter as his finest hour for the club.

Ron Greenwood, seemingly unflappable and unemotional, made another strange and slightly ungenerous comment given the circumstances, 'We could have done this sort of thing before. Martin Peters could have scored six goals against Sheffield Wednesday but didn't get one!'

It was a great win, but not, according to John, the cause of inordinate celebration. In the sixties, as far as the West Ham players were concerned, when the game was over, it was over.

In them days, when we lost, it wasn't the end of the world. Most of them boys who were at West Ham were just like schoolboys really. You play your game,

Highbury Corner.

you win, lose or draw, and as soon as you got outside of that ground you forgot about it. Some people went up the pub, some went out for a meal, others did this and that but that was it.

Appropriately Mary Hopkin was at the top of what was then known as 'The Hit Parade' with *Those Were The Days*. A gallon of petrol cost 5s 10d and the TV comedy *Dad's Army* had just started.

A body is a given life from the midst of nothingness. Is this thing, where noth-ingness is the meaning of the phrase 'Form is emptiness'.

That all things are provided for by nothingness is the meaning of the phrase 'Emptiness is form'.

The way of the Samurai is that one should not think that these are separate things.

    Hagakure, The Book of the Samurai – Yamamoto Tsunetomo

8

For the Record

'Timing is all important...I have always been a believer in hitting the ball firmly.'
(The Strategy of Soccer – Johnny Byrne)

Although he would refuse to see himself as any kind of a groundbreaker, it was only towards the end of John's career that other black players started to be seen in First Division football. On 2 April 1970 Charlo played his last game for West Ham, a 2-2 draw against the mighty Leeds side of that time. Significantly, with Clyde Best also in the starting XI it was the first time two black players had played together for the West Ham first team. The big Bermudan international scored the Hammers' first goal.

John played 132 games alongside Bobby Moore in defence of West Ham's goal – a combination of finesse and force, of art and power, speed and guile. But both men could read the game: Bobby was like an academic, generating a constant analysis of the situation, constantly looking at the field like a three-dimensional chess board that leads to a goal, entrancing would-be interlopers into his penalty area to give up possession. John was more instinctive, with an East End knack of looking every way at once. Sensitive to the position and movement of the foe, he was swift to chop down their progress with no regard for reputation, and charge along the wing sending in deadly accurate crosses at deadlier velocity. In fact, his most numerous victims were probably the brain cells of those on the end of the 'missile' passes he sent into opponent's penalty areas.

John's overall first-team match record is telling:

Season	Played	Won	Lost	Drawn	For	Against
1962/63	1	0	1	0	0	1
1963/64	2	1	0	1	7	4
1964/65	1	0	1	0	0	4
1965/66	36	16	11	9	66	56
1966/67	35	14	15	6	70	60
1967/68	23	6	14	3	41	49
1968/69	39	12	10	17	65	47
1969/70	5	2	2	1	7	7

Clyde Best out-jumps them all. His teammate Tommy Taylor, Dave Webb of Chelsea and Geoff Hurst are also in the frame.

In John's most active period, West Ham's record without Charlo in the line-up was as follows:

Season	Played	Won	Lost	Drawn	For	Against
1965/66	26	9	11	6	50	53
1966/67	15	4	7	4	30	38
1967/68	25	12	6	7	28	27
1968/69	9	4	3	2	19	13
1969/70	40	11	18	11	49	53

At first sight these figures seem to reveal little. However, John played 133 games between the 1965/66 and 1968/69 seasons and when one looks at goal averages and differences during this period, an indication of the effect of his presence in the West Ham side is suggested:

Season	Games John played		Games John did not play	
	Goal ave.	Goal diff.	Goal ave.	Goal diff.
1965/66	1.18	+10	0.94	−3
1966/67	1.16	+10	0.78	−8
1967/68	0.84	−8	1.04	+1
1968/69	1.38	+18	1.45	+6
Overall	1.14	+30	1.05	−4

Whilst the effect of John's being in the West Ham team is not revealed in the overall percentage of success (based on 2 points for a win, 1 for a draw and none for a loss, consistent with Football League rules of the time, although the above figures include cup matches), there was a 48.7% success rate without John and a 49.6% rating with him in the side. Goal average and difference figures demonstrate that, in the main and overall, the Hammers scored more goals when Charlo played, the team's victories were more emphatic, draws were higher scoring and there was more of a reply in defeat. This suggests that a certain type of spirit was stirred when John Charles entered the fray. With Charlo protecting and prompting, a sense of adventure was evoked in the ranks of the Irons, perhaps based on a feeling of greater security, 'commando' attitude, or both. These were the games when the claret-and-blue buccaneers swashbuckled and caroused and ran at their adversaries with an ethos matching the social relations that dominated the club at the time, the collective and connective relationships of young men who had played on and off the field together. They were more an East End gang than a team, more a Cockney Comanche war-party than the usual mercenary brigade of football journeymen. The games John played in included a 7-0 demolition of Leeds United in November 1966, part of an 8-day, 3-game, 17-goal party. The first leg was the Bonfire Night 6-1 rout of Fulham, then the Peacocks were crushed before the Hammers beat Spurs on their own turf, 3-4. A bizarre 5-5 draw at Stamford Bridge followed a month later. As detailed above, Charlo was also a member of the side who notched up the club's record-equalling 8-0 thrashing of Sunderland in October 1968. Like the first British European Cup-winning team, Glasgow Celtic, all of whom were born within twenty miles of Celtic Park, the West Ham side of the sixties had grown up together; they understood each other, sang the same songs and laughed at the same jokes. In fact, during his entire seven-year first-team career John played with only forty-eight other professionals. The number was less than this if one tightens one's focus to his peak years. The names of those he lined up alongside read like a 'Who's Who' of West Ham United and also part of English football in the mid- to late sixties:

George Andrew	Ken Brown	Jimmy Greaves	Colin Mackleworth
Peter Bennett	Jack Burkett	Peter Grotier	Keith Miller
Clyde Best	Denis Burnett	Trevor Hartley	Bobby Moore
Dave Bickles	Johnny Byrne	Paul Heffer	Martin Peters
Jimmy Bloomfield	Roger Cross	Bobby Howe	Eddie Presland
John Bond	John Cushley	Geoff Hurst	Harry Redknapp
Billy Bonds	Trevor Dawkins	Joe Kirkup	Brian Rhodes
Ronnie Boyce	Brian Dear	Bill Kitchener	Alan Sealey
Eddie Bovington	Alan Dickie	Frank Lampard	Tony Scott
Peter Brabrook	Doug Eadie	Lawrie Leslie	John Sissons
Martin Britt	Peter Eustace	Jimmy Lindsay	Jim Standen
Trevor Brooking	Bobby Ferguson	John Lyall	Alan Stevenson

Alvin Martin beating Dai Davies of Wrexham at Upton Park.

The above cavalcade is no mean bunch. It includes all the members of the FA Cup and European Cup Winners Cup teams, around a dozen players who had or would win full caps and many more who had represented their nation at youth and Under-23 levels, as well as others who had gained selection for international squads. In his way, John was as good as any and better than many, and more than deserves to be numbered in their ranks.

John had been out of football for nearly five years when West Ham again made the FA Youth Cup Final.

1975 – West Ham's fourth FA Youth Cup final: hard luck Alvin

Among the ranks of the young Hammers were Alvin Martin, who was to be one of the longest serving players at Upton Park in the modern era, the current Charlton Athletic manager Alan Curbishley, Paul Brush, who would become boss at Brisbane Road, and Geoff Pike, whom John Lyall would name as one of the first players he would have in his ideal West Ham side (see *Days of Iron*). This time the Hammers' opponents were Ipswich Town, the club that had won the Cup for the first time two years previously.

Already assured of the South-east Counties title, the Tractor Boys made a dream start to the final, grabbing 2 goals in the first half-hour of the first leg in front of over 10,000 of the claret and blue 'faithful' at the Boleyn Ground. Although physically stronger, Ipswich were rocked by West Ham's more direct play at the beginning of the second half and in the fifty-second minute, Terry Sharpe scrambled the ball over the visitors' goal line. However, the Ipswich back four then demonstrated how they had managed to concede no more than a single goal in the competition prior to the final. On the platform of a secure defence, the East Anglians forced a third goal with just three minutes of the match remaining.

In the second leg at Portman Road, the Irons were overpowered and were well beaten 2-0. The result brought a great deal of satisfaction to a crowd of over 16,000 Ipswich fans who had seen their first team beaten by the Hammers in a rain-soaked FA Cup semi-final at Stamford Bridge three weeks earlier. That year, of course, West Ham went on to lift the famous old trophy.

> 'Once you have accomplished the move don't rest on your laurels. A moment's relaxation may allow another opponent to get in a tackle.'
>
> *(The Strategy of Soccer* – Johnny Byrne)

9

What is Racism?

'I am a great believer in enthusiasm. Of course, we shall never reach perfection. We shall always be stretching for further achievements. A show of nerves, or indecision can have a bad influence on teammates and will lead to disaster.'

(*The Strategy of* Soccer – Johnny Byrne)

From the very start of John's career at Upton Park it seems there was some consciousness of potential racism, the young Charlo being the first black player at the club. Ted Fenton made an early attempt at anti-racist practice: 'When I was taken on the ground staff, Ted told me that I would get called a few names, but to keep kicking 'em.'

There is little doubt that John did experience forms of racism, but he did not seem to notice, or more likely chose to ignore the more covert/institutional forms of discrimination. He told me about his trial to join the ground staff at Upton Park (see p.35). His friend and fellow defender, Peter Turner, failed to be selected. However, Turner, who later entered football obscurity by way of Highbury, was selected for the English School Boys. Charlie Green, who was also at that West Ham trial and was a life-long friend of John's from the days when they played together as schoolboys, told me: 'John Charles definitely missed out on playing for England Boys. He was the best defender in the country. I think it was just his colour that went against him. It was the time. He was the best around. Without a shadow of a doubt, when the probables played the possibles he was the best defender.'

John also had to contend with the force of racism when he was prevented from taking part in West Ham's 1963 triumph in the American Challenge Cup because of the trouble accompanying the challenges to segregation in the USA at that time (see p.45). The club thought, in the circumstances, that it was better to leave John at home. However, the players that won the tournament included the core of the sides that would contest and win the FA Cup in 1964 and the European Cup Winners Cup in the following year. This group also contained the four players who were chosen for the initial England World Cup squad, three of whom played in the victorious 1966 side. John's non-inclusion in West Ham's 'American Odyssey' of 1963 because of racism on a massive cultural scale may well have had a profound and lasting effect on his career and future life.

Three Hammers – Bobby Moore, Geoff Hurst and Martin Peters – line up at the start of the 1966 World Cup Final, which was a wonderful achievement – but West Ham might have had five players in that England side.

I never remember any real racism

As John broke into the first team at Upton Park there were very few black players in League football. It might be expected that, as the first black player to make West Ham's first team and one of the first to break through in London football, John would have experienced a level of racism, both from crowds and other players. However, this was not the case according to John:

> *I never remember any real racism, certainly not from other players at West Ham or our crowd. Maybe some players respond to it too quickly and become a target when everyone knows it winds them up. If they'd just keep playing they would stop. I was always detailed to mark the likes of Greaves and Best. They would call out, 'unload him, kick 'em'.*

However, some fans remember the occasional visiting player looking to goad John through the use of racist remarks, but he seemed, for the most part, to react in the manner he describes above, or act on the advice of his first manager, Ted Fenton. For example, a supporter who witnessed the Red spring massacre of 1966/67 (see p.75) recalled, 'There was a blood bath on the terraces and Charlo twatted Dennis Law – for which he was sent off...some said Law called him a black bastard, I would never know.'

For all this, in the main John did not appear to see these kind of remarks as a problem, in that their purpose was clear and that they were exceptional. He told me, 'You got the odd "black bastard", but that never worried me. But my mum would go mad if anyone called me a black bastard, she said she was the only one who could call me that. And she'd say "He's not a bastard."' John laughed at the memory.

In one conversation with John I brought up the accusation that some black players, for example Les Ferdinand and John Barnes in their respective autobiographies, have accused West Ham fans of being racist. John's response was typically forthright:

> *Barnes is a nutter then ain't he? Saying the West Ham crowd are a racist club! I never had none of it at West Ham. None at all. That Inter City Firm all used to drink in Lampard's pub at Plaistow, The Brit. They was alright, always good with me. I was a greengrocer then, there was no problem. It's a bit of a myth. I used to serve Bobby Barnes* [a member of the 'second generation' of black West Ham players] *on our stall. He never had a problem. Old Jimmy Frith* [a long-serving coach at West Ham] *has been there for years. He's been there for a good thirty years, he's older than me, he's got to be sixty-something. He never had any problems with that sort of thing. No. The idea that West Ham fans are racist is rubbish!*

Whilst John Charles might have had few problems with West Ham supporters, it seems he did experience racism away from Upton Park. Charlie Green recalled: 'He took some abuse on the field. The team had come back from playing away, up North I think. John got back in the evening and he met me in the Black Lion at Plaistow. We went up the Rook, down in Leytonstone, cos there used to be a disco there, and John told me that he'd had bananas thrown at him. They did that with Clyde Best as well. John was upset about that. I said, "I'm going to give you a very solid bit of advice about that. Let's get pissed." And we did. We got wrecked. We got totally wrecked that night.'

Talking about other black players who followed Charlo to Upton Park, John recalled: 'We were playing a reserve game and this Ade Coker was playing.' Coker was a talented player that Greenwood brought to West Ham from Nigeria. Ade was one of the first African players to play in the Football League. John continued:

> *Me, Johnny Cushley and Deary were playing I remember. Anyway, Ade was useless. He never done a thing. At half time he's holding his stomach and he's talking to Robby Jenkins* [the club physiotherapist at the time] *and Rob asked him, 'What's the matter with yer Ade?' And he went, 'I got de…stom…och… up…sets.* [John giggled.] *Well, the whole dressing room just collapsed cos of the way he said it, because that's the way he used to talk an' all.*

This in itself could easily be construed as a form of racism, but it seems more consistent with the West Ham 'piss-take' culture that affected every player at the club. For example, Charlie Green told me: 'In terms of drinking, Bobby Moore had hollow legs. He also had hollow pockets. It was murder getting him to pay for a round. Once I was

Clyde Best challenges Manchester United and England 'keeper Alex Stepney at Upton Park, 2 September 1972.

WEST HAM UNITED F.C.

BOLEYN GROUND GREEN STREET, UPTON PARK, LONDON, E.13

ORIENT Colts

LONDON YOUTH CUP - Senior Section : Semi - Final

MONDAY 1 MARCH 1971 at 7.30 p.m.

WEST HAM UNITED Youth XI		ORIENT Colts	
1	Mervyn Day	1	Mike O'Shaughnassy
2	Chris Kinnear	2	Stephen Trice
3	Ray Fulton	3	John Taplin
4	John Watson	4	John South
5	Tony Marchant	5	Paul Harris
6	Kevin Lock (capt.)	6	Alan Durrant
7	John Ayris	7	Gerald Sullivan
8	Jimmy Brown	8	Malcolm Philby
9	Ade Coker	9	Ian Philby
10	Paul Gregory	10	Martin Binks
11	Joe Durrell	11	David Staines
12	Gary Yallop	12	Martin Littlefield

There will be extra time if the scores are level after 90 minutes

REFEREE: Mr. B. LIVESEY
LINESMEN: *Red Flag*: Mr. L. WILLIE
Orange Flag: Mr. K. LUGG

OFFICIAL PROGRAMME: 1½p   No. 41

Ade Coker – West Ham Colt.

in a group out drinking with him and one of us said really quickly, "Bobby Moore captain of West Ham captain of England OBE…buy a fucking round!"'

I didn't know they were different colours!

As in his football career, racism does not appear to have been a major theme in the life of John's family. Carol, thinking about this, told me: 'We've been together for forty years and I can count on one hand the racial abuse that we've had. We didn't even call it a mixed marriage. It was never ever a problem.' John added:

> *You didn't have none of that. I suppose because I played for West Ham people knew who I was and we got left alone. What is racism? Well, what is it? When I was a kid I never ever had any black friends in my little area. There wasn't hardly any there. I grew up and then the black kids were only youngsters, all flash ones. I walk along the road, see a group of white lads and get looked at and I walk round the corner and a load of black lads look at me just the same – I think gawd blimey!*

Carol: 'We stayed in our circle. We never had no trouble. The main thing I get and my kids get is, "Oh we're not referring to you because you're different" – but we're not different, we're all the same. I say to myself "Grrr". But the media hype up the race thing – a crowd of boys go out for a drink they can be a crowd of black boys or a crowd of white boys, and cos there's a fight why does it have to be about that?'

> John: *I've been in a pub and all me mates are white…there might have been a crowd of black guys in there, I've walked by 'em and they've all sort of growled at me for being with whites. I've thought, 'Oh dear, I've got to get out of here'.*

Carol confirmed John's perception: 'We've felt those type of vibes many a time and thought, "We'd better get out of here".' John went on:

> *The women are a bit funny, but I don't get near 'em. I've seen bits and pieces and felt 'caal'! You might get some comments in a pub, about blacks, but they'd turn around and say 'Oh not you John. That's nothing against you John. I wouldn't say nothing to you'. I'd say, 'Alright'.*

We got on to talk about the case of Stephen Lawrence and John concluded: 'If it's a white bloke who gets in trouble with a group of black kids you don't see nothing.' John and Carol's eldest son Keith confirmed John and Carol's feeling that racism was never really an issue for the family. He thought hard before he told me that, 'Sometimes you'd get names at school, but we never really had any trouble.'

And according to the Charles' youngest son, Mitchell: 'We never had any trouble with racism. I grew up, even though me dad's black, not knowing it. In my eyes, I didn't see other people seeing him as black. Didn't have a problem with it'. Deana, Mitchell's wife, confirmed her husband's perspective: 'It is funny, because I've been places with Mitch where people have gone, "Fucking black bastards", and it's like they're not talking about anyone to do with your family. If you say, "Hold on", they say, "Oh no, not them." It's like they don't even see the colour. I've been with his friends and I thought, "Aye, aye, you going on?"'

Mitchell agreed, 'Yeah, some of my mates were quite…' Deana prompted, 'Racist.' Mitchell continued, 'Yeah, but not to us.'

It also seems that the family did not experience overt discrimination or prejudice relating to John and Carol being in what society used to call a 'mixed marriage' in the sixties. Mitchell told me, 'Never once did I get affected by mum and dad being in a mixed-race marriage. Wouldn't even have known it. Nothing at school. Nothing ever.' Deana: 'It's the same for Nancy, my friend, Mitch's cousin. She's from Collier Row, and that's a really predominantly white area. She was the only person in her school from a mixed race family, no-one ever said anything.

Lesley, John and Carol's daughter, told me: 'This is a really stupid story. But I didn't know they were different colours! You don't see it. It's only when people point it out to you that there's a problem. At the end of the day it wasn't a problem to me. But the sad thing was that I was about eleven, I'll never forget it. My class at school was mostly white. There was Julian Saunders who was black and there was Paul Samidas who was Indian and me! And Julian Saunders come up to me one day, we was talking about something or other and he turned round to me and said, "But you're the same as me!" And I went, "How do you work that out?" He said, "But your dad's black!" That really threw me because I'd never really looked at my mum and dad as being black and white. Cos they're just my parents! It took me eleven years to work it out! [This still seems to amuse Lesley.] But my kids don't see colour unless it's pointed out. That's what I hate about racism. It comes from the parents at the end of the day. A few years back, Jessica [Lesley's eldest daughter] and me were sitting on the floor drawing, me and Rita [John's sister] it was round me mum's. And Jessica said to Rita, "Why is your hand that colour?" And Rita said "It's the same colour as yer grandad's." Jess said "No it's not."'

Rita (who was with Lesley at the time we were speaking), added: 'She didn't twig. As time went by she asked me again. And I said, "Cos our dad lived in a country that was really hot and that's why we're brown." But she'd not noticed it before. You don't see it. I never saw it. It wasn't a problem until senior school. Because people want to know what you are. When me and John was at school there was us two and another kid and someone said, "John's black ain't he." Mum went up the school.' Rita laughed at the memory.

He was more of a cockney than we was!

It is, of course, possible that John, his family and all the other black Hammers I have spoken with over the last five years (around thirty as part of another project) who have confirmed John's perspective, have got it wrong, or were just in some kind of state of denial, but this would be a very disparaging and disrespectful conclusion to reach. John, Carol, Lesley, Rita, Keith and Mitchell and all the other players I spoke to were bright, intelligent and articulate people. They were clear about their feelings and memories and the major forms of racism that effect people's lives seem, as in John's case, to be institutional in nature.

Reg Leseurf confirmed John's view. He told me, 'They didn't give 'em stick like they do now. John always said he never had any trouble with any of that.' Brian Dear also backed Charlo's contention about the lack of racism at Upton Park when he said, 'None of us would have stood for that. But it was never a problem.'

Perhaps Charlie Green and Reg Leseurf summed up the whole situation most succinctly. Charlie told me, 'When you go round yer mate's house and he's black and his mum's white you go, "That's unusual, come on, let's go and play football." Colour didn't come into it. The only time I see him upset was when he'd had bananas thrown at him. He was me mate. You didn't notice things like colour with yer mates!'

Reg added, maybe most tellingly, 'He was more of a cockney than we was!' As always, Charlie had the last word, 'Course he was!'

Football racism

Given the nature of the debate around racism over the past three decades or so, the perspective developed in this chapter is perhaps surprising, particularly in the context of the sixties, a time before a consciousness of race relations and equal opportunities became imbedded in British social policy and the consciousness of everyday life. John and Carol's son, Mitchell, told me: 'I was listening to a programme on Radio London a few months ago and they were talking about racism in football. One of the presenters was a black guy, he was saying how bad it was. I phoned up and said me dad played in the sixties and never found anything like that. The presenter bloke just laughed at me as if I was lying!'

This obviously surprised and puzzled Mitchell more than angered him. For him and his family the truth of their lives, their experience, is denied by a media that seem intent on highlighting and maybe exaggerating a negative image of football fans and players, in particular those from working-class backgrounds. This makes someone like me, who has talked, listened to, laughed and cried with John's family for nearly half a decade and who has interviewed dozens of black players on this subject, most of whom have shared the attitude that was expressed by the Charles family, question exactly what agenda the popular media has in emphasising and constantly elaborating the alleged, seemingly profound, racism propagated by certain players and fans.*

---

* Here I am talking about the English situation. It is understood that recent incidents of racism when English clubs have visited European grounds have been profound and unacceptable. However, the institutional question is still pertinent. Why do English clubs continue to play in such atmospheres? Why is it that when players are racially abused, teams are not simply hauled off the park? The excuse is that this would be giving way to racists, but is it likely that clubs are much more preoccupied with the impact on their finances and are prepared to place their players in the firing line as long as the price is right? One only has to look at the derisory fines given to European clubs whose fans have exhibited racism to understand the dynamics of the situation. The English football authorities and, latterly, UEFA have never shown the definite institutional motivation to combat racism that it would take to kick clubs out of competitions when racism has been prevalent at matches. The rules of the game allow for a player to be dismissed from a match when they have illegally impeded another physically, but when a player is impeded by the racist taunts and abuse of maybe thousands of people, the punishment has been no more than a cursory financial penalty that is a monetary raindrop in football's economic ocean.

Perhaps this exercise in demonisation is meaningless. Maybe it is a knee-jerk reaction or purely an attempt to create news. But it may also be a tactic; a means of deflection that takes up the space available (at the same time demonstrating 'concern') that effectively prevents the asking of a number of difficult questions. For example:

How does racism in football really affect black people involved in the game?

How does it prevent non-whites from developing their involvement in management and/or administration?

How does it stop people from ethnic minorities from becoming a part of the football industry at the point of delivery and/or promotion?

Given the relatively high numbers of black professionals playing at the very top of the game now for more than thirty years, why are there so few black coaches, board members and managers within the upper echelons of football?

How many black people are employed at executive level by the FA?

Why are players with the experience and knowledge of, for example, Ian Wright, spending their time on demeaning activities like dancing about like a cockerel in TV advertisements for cook-in-the-packet chicken, whilst the English national team, which he was so proud to be part of, cannot find the net?

Why are leading clubs setting up nursery facilities in Australia and nurturing American talent? Both of these countries have come on leaps and bounds in terms of their 'soccer development' over the last decade or two, but they are not leading football nations. However they are, for different reasons, two places where white players dominate the game. It is strange that leading clubs are investing money so far from home, when in Britain we now have a tradition of football skill across the ethnic landscape, but most impressively, in terms of percentages, within our indigenous black and Asian populations. For all this, England seems to be becoming the home of the 'socceroo' and the football cowboy, even though the USA and, in particular, Australia cannot compare with performances of the top four or five African nations over the last ten years or so.

Given all this, why, to use an expression deriving from the days of slavery, are the fans the constant 'whipping boys' in the debate relating to racism?

Maybe it is time the liberal, mainly white, mainly middle-class sociology students and the predominantly middle-aged academics extracted themselves from the stands and got themselves into the boardrooms of football? Perhaps it would be useful for them to spend a little less time endlessly analysing for offence the songs sung by supporters that have hardly been heard at Upton Park, Highbury, Old Trafford or any venue of note in years*, and give more effort to asking some awkward questions of those who, own, run and define football?

---

* A while ago I came across a piece of research that had it that 'Knees Up Muvver Brown' was sexist, that the *Hokey-Cokey* discriminated against people who were 'other able', and the singing of *No Regrets* to a French player and the relating of the tune to the *Dam Busters* to German fans were both acts of 'racism' (Germany and France are 'nations' – there are no German or French 'races').

As things stand there is what seems like a divide and rule situation pertaining. Black people with a passionate interest and love for the game have in reality little alternative in terms of addressing the institutional racism within football except to turn to and use the existing structures set up for that purpose. Unfortunately, these are often funded by the same institutions that maintain what is effectively a glass ceiling (as far as black people are concerned) within the game; the clubs, the FA, UEFA and so on. This being the case, racism within football is put squarely on the shoulders of the supporters, those who give up the most for the game, but who have the least control/power in terms of the soccer industry. So, the final equation places blacks, devoted to the game and the pursuit of justice, on the same side as the organisations that, albeit unconsciously, continue to preside over forms of institutional racism. On the other side are those who pay to watch and support teams and players, no matter what. In the long term this risks the generation of mutual resentment, a hint of which may have been felt by that radio presenter referred to above (p.99) and certainly Mitchell when he telephoned that radio programme (ibid.).

'A hasty, ill-judged clearance so often results in the opposition coming right back to the attack, whereas a good kick can put the opposing team at panic stations.'
(*The Strategy of Soccer* – Johnny Byrne)

John led. Many others followed and are pictured on the following pages. Andy Impey and Hammer-to-be Titi Camara are pictured here.

Marc Viven Foe.

Above left: Shaka Hislop.

Above right: Paul Ince.

Right: George Parris.

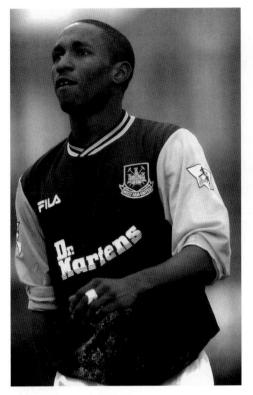

Above left: Jermain Defoe.

Above right: David James.

Right: Paulo Wanchope.

Opposite: Freddie Kanoute.

Titi Camara.

Samassi Abou.

10

We Went from the Club to the Pub

'Conserve your energy; never chase hopeless balls; and never think your stamina is endless. Put everything into your game, but do it sensibly.'

(*The Strategy of Soccer* – Johnny Byrne)

It was not John's race or colour that would be the accompanying theme of his career and it was not racism that would undermine his potential. As John became established in the West Ham Division One side, taking his place along side Johnnie Byrne, Geoff Hurst, Martin Peters and Bobby Moore, the Hammers looked like it had a powerful side, but the club was never really able to build on the successes of the early sixties. When thinking about this John commented:

Maybe the team didn't build on their success in the sixties because we were always on the piss. We went from the club to the pub. I was part of a hard drinking crowd, Brian Dear, Bobby Moore, Eddie Bovington, and Budgie. Mooro was a good player, but he was a bit slow. But he could read the game a bit. He could read what people were going to do. That's what made him a good player. He was as good as gold on the field and off the field he was a piss-head. [John chortled.] *He liked a gin and tonic.*

Carol interjected, 'He was a lovely man.' John continued:

He liked a lager too. You couldn't get him drunk! He was one of the best drinkers I knew. He was on par with Oliver Reed! Gawd he could drink! He was a quiet bloke but entertaining. There are times when I've gone down the Retreat at Chigwell, and I've thought, Mooro's car's outside his house, I'll drop in and see him. We'd pop in sometimes and he'd get the beers out of the fridge and we'd forget the 'Retreat'. We'd sit and have a chat. Then the next morning he'd come in and say, 'Do you know we drank about a crate and half of them lagers last night?'

A culture of drink

John went on to elaborate on West Ham's and football's drinking culture of the 1960s:

> *It was amazing. In them days, no-one was really fit. You'd get the odd few but everyone liked a drink, it wasn't just West Ham. It was footballer's lives in the sixties. 'Win, draw or lose we're on the booze!' You didn't even think about it. It was second nature. When players get pulled up for drinking now it's nothing. I spilt more down me tie!*

John chuckled. Carol added, 'We all knew when to stop.' John grabbed his chance, 'Yeah, when we fell over.' They both laughed. 'If you wanted an alcoholic you could go round to Charlo's.' He laughed ironically. 'If you want someone to do the nutcracker suite get him as well.' John broke into a rain of smiles.

It is certain that a drinking tradition was well established at West Ham by the early sixties and that John seemed to be part of it from his debut in 1963. It is true that alcohol was part of the game at that time, but at Upton Park it seemed far more deeply entrenched than other clubs in the top flight. Charlo's friend, Reg Lerseurf, recalled: 'They used to go drinking. I'd got married at nineteen. So I never got involved with the drinking. Just as well, it would have killed me. I used to see John occasionally, but I was working on the ground as an electrician. I was too lazy to be a pro. I didn't like the training. Chas Green met with John at the dogs or whatever.'

1963 was the same year that John won his FA Youth Cup winner's medal and broke into the England Youth side. He recalled:

> *It was before my first game, the one against Blackburn, that my bother-in-law asked me to come for a drink, down Grange Road where my Mum lived. I had two pints, and that's the least I've ever had in a pub. [He laughed ironically.] When we lived on the Barking Road, John Cushely was a good mate, and Dave Bickles. We went to the Retreat after training at Chigwell. Greenwood never seemed to notice. We used to hide our cars round the back. Then we'd go to the Slaters Arms, a right old dive of a pub in Romford, but they did afters. We'd go to and from away matches to places like Newcastle by first-class train. By the end of the journey home the bottles of miniatures were piled up in a big heap and we'd thrown half out of the window.*

Charlie Green confirmed the kind of 'brotherhood of alcohol' that revolved around the West Ham team of the sixties: 'I come out of West Ham and I got hold of a job that paid a few bob. The 'in' place was the Rodings, at Abridge, that was *the* restaurant. Mooro, Hursty and Peters, Alan Ball, Sean Connery, all the stars used to go down there and if you had a couple of bob you could go down there. So I could afford to stay in John's company. So we'd see more of each other that way.

'Hursty was a good boozer, not so much Peters. Lampard was another good boozer. But it weren't every night of the week. It was weekends after a game. The Black Lion was another "in" place. It used to be a laugh and that's when John used to relax most.

You could go in there without fans and autographs and people getting on their case hardly ever discussing football. He knew that I knew that he didn't want to talk about football after a game. In yer head, in yer face all the time.

'We used to go to away games in groups, eight, ten-handed. We went for a reason. We'd stay in the same hotel as the players and after the game we'd go out for a jolly. We'd meet up with them at about midnight, they'd been out for a meal and you'd be up to five, six, seven in the morning. Birds were like bees to a honey pot. The team were on the piss before and after games. It's the same now, look at it. Woodgate, Dennis Wise. The only manager who had any sort of control was Brian Clough. He put up curfews. He was the only manager in Division One to try to install a rigorous regime. Even he was banging his head against a brick wall most of the time.

'Friday nights down the Roding before matches were the thing. You never booked yer table to ten o'clock at night. Beer, Champagne, you'd be there to 3, 4, 5 a.m. They were all there, Mooro and that. Pissed! [Charlie laughed.] He was never keen to keen to get his money out. Bobby Moore wasn't a person to rush to the bar and buy a round. He was renowned for not doing that.'

In his autobiography, Bobby Moore remembered being with John and John Cushley in 1967 in the United States. According to Moore, they were so drunk at three in the afternoon that they were not even able to maintain contact with their beds which they tried to collapse onto. They all crashed to the floor in total inebriation. Sadly, happenings of this type were to be the seeds of John's personal demise. But it took time to kick in and it was not until he had left football for a good while that the consequences of his earlier activity were fully felt.

Into the maze

In the years straight after he left football it seemed that drinking was the main legacy the game left him with. John's son, Keith, told me, 'I always remember him down the market and the pubs. I was always outside the Brit.' He smiled, satirising the tedium many of us have experienced waiting for adults involved in adult pursuits. ' "We going home yet?" Mum's always stuck by him. Me mum used to work on the stall as well, lifting sacks of potatoes. She was strong. He always had a bit of rage inside him when he'd been on the booze. Everyone's mate down the pub then come home and have a ding-dong with me mum, but that was dad and that was how everyone was then, everyone did it. Nowadays it would be women's lib and all that malarkey, but that was how it was. Alf Garnett times basically. Other families down the street were going for one another. He used to shout and holler but he never really raised his hand to me. I just used to stand to attention.' Tittering, Keith mimed exaggerated obedience.

Mitchell, John's youngest son, also had memories of his father's relationship with alcohol: 'I was probably closer to me mum, but there weren't much in it at all. Probably where he was up the pub a lot. [He laughed.] But he was fine. He used to come home when he was sloshed and he was sometimes happy, sometimes miserable. He was probably Jack the lad when he was out with his mates and everything. When he got home he weren't horrible but he wasn't as entertaining, although he was sometimes.'

John Charles at Upton Park by Stephen Marsh.

However, John was a man who looked for humour and his drinking escapades were a rich source of amusement. For example, Mitchell told me: 'Some of the stories he told me. He was in a pub called the Four Sisters, up in North London, Islington way, Kentish Town something like that. When he was going up the fruit and veg market, he used to go drinking with all the greengrocers whatever. They'd start about four in the morning. The lorries used to get loaded up and they'd pay blokes to drive the lorries home and they'd go out for a beer. One day, I can't believe how he got away with it, they were all in the pub, me dad, Johnny Snipe, Danny I think and a few others and me dad's gone out the pub and he's come back with a midget! He's nicked a midget from out in the street. [Mitch giggled as he stood to act out the story.] It's so out of order really. He picked him up and he said, "You're staying with us. Give this man a beer." They wouldn't let him go! They basically kidnapped a midget and went on the piss with him all day. At the end they all parted ways and the little bloke had a great time. The old man actually picked him up and he walked in the pub with him under his arm!'

1981: West Ham's fifth FA Youth Cup final: welcome Bobby Barnes

West Ham were once again drawn at home in the first leg of the FA Youth Cup Final. A crowd of 13,400 were at Upton Park to see the first all-London Final between the Hammers and Tottenham Hotspur, who, like Ipswich six seasons earlier, were going for the Cup and League double.

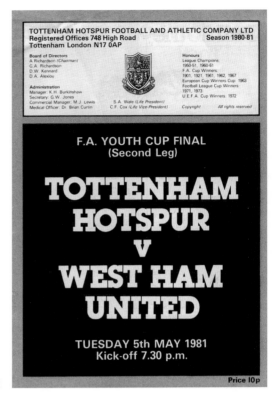

TOTTENHAM HOTSPUR FOOTBALL AND ATHLETIC COMPANY LTD
Registered Offices 748 High Road   Season 1980-81
Tottenham London N17 0AP

Board of Directors
A Richardson *(Chairman)*
G.A. Richardson
D.W. Kennard
D.A. Alexiou

Administration
Manager: K.H. Burkinshaw
Secretary: G.W. Jones
Commercial Manager: M.J. Lewis   S.A. Wale *(Life President)*
Medical Officer: Dr. Brian Curtin   C.F. Cox *(Life Vice-President)*

Honours
League Champions:
1950-51, 1960-61
F.A. Cup Winners:
1901, 1921, 1961, 1962, 1967
European Cup Winners Cup: 1963
Football League Cup Winners:
1971, 1973
U.E.F.A. Cup Winners: 1972

Copyright   *All rights reserved*

F.A. YOUTH CUP FINAL
(Second Leg)

TOTTENHAM HOTSPUR
v
WEST HAM UNITED

TUESDAY 5th MAY 1981
Kick-off 7.30 p.m.

Price 10p

Spurs are beaten!

West Ham took the lead just before the quarter of an hour mark when Wayne Reader headed home a Mark Schiavi cross. Further fine saves by Tony Parkes prevented the Irons from extending their lead, until seven minutes before full time Bobby Barnes scored from the penalty spot after Schiavi had been tripped in the area.

Thousands of Hammers' fans were in the 13,765 spectators at White Hart Lane twelve days after the first leg. West Ham should have taken the lead just before the break but Glen Burvill somehow managed to screw the ball high and wide from almost under the crossbar.

This miss looked like it was proving to be costly when Terry Gibson scored for Spurs just after the interval. With just ten minutes of the game remaining, a perfect cross by Barnes was knocked back by Paul Allen to Steve Milton, but his header from close-range missed the target. (Paul Allen would later become the youngest player to turn out in an FA Cup final when West Ham beat Arsenal in 1980.)

In pouring rain, West Ham soaked up the final Spurs pressure to end up worthy winners by a 2-1 aggregate, to bring the Trophy back to Upton Park for the second time. Amongst the lads who played for West Ham over the two legs of the final, were four young black Hammers, Bobby Barnes, Keith McPherson, Chris Ampofo and skipper Everald La Ronde. The Irons had come a long way since John had forged the way.

The cracker factory

John told me, 'I soon had stalls all over Kent, but then they started to open the super-markets and we went skint.' He confessed: 'I was an alcoholic and in the end had a breakdown. I was so bad, once, in hospital, I dreamt I was eating my sister in a sandwich!' He laughed gently. He had started drinking more heavily as his business failed. He admitted to being terrified when he was taken into what he called 'the cracker factory', thinking that he was just going to have a check-up.

Keith told me about his experience of his father's health problems: 'I was away when he went in the mad house. I was surprised big time. He'd had his moments, shouting and rearing up, but he'd never got violent. I found out around August '94. Me mum phoned me up in Hong Kong, said, "Dad's been taken away to the nut house." I was going to come back but everyone said, "What can you do?"

'When he had his breakdown the stalls were going down the pan. It was a dying trade. His Mum, old Jessie, had just died – that was in August '94. And of course, he'd always been a boozer, but it all just got to him in the end. He was only having a pint or so down the pub and he was staggering home. That wasn't like him. It had got him. He'd really lost it. He was away for about six months and he was getting treatment, medication, for about a year and a half after that.'

Mitchell recalled: 'He was sectioned, taken away when I was in Australia. I went there on 31 May 1994. I didn't know what had happened! I phoned up, apparently he was hearing things on the phone. I'd just got to Australia, didn't tell anyone I was going, and said [Mitch broke into a broad Australian accent], "G'day mate, how yer doing?" He's going "Who's that? Who's that?" He's already hearing voices and now he's got a mad Australian on the phone! I didn't know nothing. I was out there for a couple of months before Mum told me. Mum kept it from me for a while; she didn't tell me because she didn't want me to worry and didn't know what was going to happen, was he going to be better in a week or a month? I didn't have the cash to come home anyway.'

Charlie Green told me about how he found out about John's mental breakdown: 'I phoned Charlo after about two years of being out of touch. He didn't recognise me voice and I said, "I was the one who used to bite yer ears." He hated having his ears bit. And he said, "Charlie!" He told me that day was his fiftieth birthday. I didn't know it. It was uncanny. We were talking for ages then he told me, "I been in the bleedin' nuthouse." They did a spread about it in *The Sun*. West Ham was the cause of it, but there's plenty of players whose career ended early that didn't go that way. So other things were involved too.'

For Reg Lerseurf, part of John's problems with drink were related to his ability to sustain it financially: 'He had the money then. He was earning £75 a week as a footballer and it went up to £200 when he went on the stalls. He was earning more than Bobby Moore.' He recalled that article in *The Sun* with understandable distaste. 'It came out on his fiftieth birthday. As a double-page spread.' We talked about how after his breakdown John had been obliged to work in a supermarket and what else might have been done for him. Reg, obviously feeling strongly about the situation said, 'West Ham never had any loyalty to anyone.' We all talked about the reality of the game, that it could be seen like any other business and from one perspective it owes nothing to

Johnnie the man.

former employees. No organisation could survive if it set itself up as having an uncon-ditional welfare role in relation to ex-employees. But given the community nature of football support, West Ham's need for the same, and John's roots in that community, one can understand Reg's point of view.

Hearing of Charlo's illness, Ron Greenwood has commented: 'I'm sorry to hear about John. I'd like to wish him a very happy birthday and hope that his fortunes change for the better. He was a perfect gentleman and a good club man, steady and reliable.'

However, former playing colleagues like Ronnie Boyce, Jimmy Greaves, Frank Lampard senior and of course Brian Dear, visited John whilst he was in treatment. But it was 'Stag' who was always the most attentive. For John's son Keith, 'Brian Dear was the top man. He's stuck by dad through thick and thin since they were kids.'

I wondered what made Brian and John so close and Keith laughed, 'It was probably the drinking that brought 'em together. Everything centred round pubs, booze, laughs, jokes and all that. Deary has always been a joker, a spiteful git when he was younger.' He giggled and I could see this was meant in respect and admiration for one of John's oldest and certainly most loyal friends. 'But he's always been good.'

Recovery – I was a stranger to everyone

Following his mental health problems, John came out of hospital just before his fiftieth birthday, saying that the idea of ever touching a drink again was frightening. By now John was around 14st in weight, about 3st heavier than in his playing days. At this time John did not see much of his former West Ham colleagues, but he told me,

> *Boycey [Ronnie Boyce] has always stayed in touch. I saw him other week with Bovington. Brian Dear is as good as gold, he's been fantastic. Kenny Lynch was always okay. He lives towards the south of England, Bristol way.*

Charlo was on medication for over a year after he was discharged from hospital. The aftermath of the psychological trauma continued to have physical repercussions as John pointed out, 'Three years after the breakdown I was 16½st. I just blew up. I was nearly as big as Clyde Best!' (Best grew to almost 20st when he left football.) Carol recalled, 'John put on a lot of weight when he was ill, when he went into hospital, and what with all the medication.' Looking impishly at John she joked: 'But simple people eat a lot don't they.' John and Carol exchanged smiles and laughed.

With his brother Clive, John formed one of only six sets of brothers to play League football for West Ham. The others were Jack and George Hilsdon, Albert and Frank Denyer, Ted and Benny Fenton, David and Norman Corbett and Bill and Andy Nelson, who like Clive and John were also Canning Town boys. Clive and John played together for West Ham in the Football Combination side during most of the 1970/71 season. First making a living as a player and then as a coach, Clive had become a citizen of the United States. He was one of the leading coaches in America by the early/mid-nineties, taking the USA soccer team to the Olympics.

Carol recalled one of the last periods of time they had spent with John's 'little brother': 'Our Clive had this beautiful beach house on Cannon Beach in the States, we stayed there. Anyway, we went out one day after dinner...'

John: 'Clive always walks his dinner off.'

Carol: 'Well we walked for about two minutes and John had to sit on a bench. We walked for about an hour and half, about four miles.' John made a light-hearted excuse: 'Well it was that sand weren't it! You needed stamina to walk on that!' Carol went on: 'When we came back he was still sitting on the bench. Clive said he looked like Forrest Gump.' They both giggled.

John seemed to see his malaise starting when he had to give up football. He told me:

> *I loved playing for West Ham, but I got injured and couldn't get over it, so I turned to drink. I was an alcoholic and in the end had a breakdown. If I had to do it all again I wouldn't have drunk. I'd have kept myself right fit. Because the money they're getting now is beyond belief. And to play the game you've gotta be fit.*

However, John's problems cannot just be blamed on the 'West Ham drink culture' or his departure from the game. The decline of the market trade, which was part of the

Canning Town boys, brother Hammers – Clive and John Charles.

national financial slump that happened around the same time, was also a factor. Discussing this led our conversation onto politics. John told me: 'I've not got one bit of politics in me. None at all! I just can't stand it. If I voted I used to vote Conservative.' Carol interjected: 'Once you voted – once in his life! Even looking at 'em, looking at these politicians on the telly! Or hear 'em joking in front of each other!' John concluded in exasperation, 'Politics…cor! Unbelievable… and they're all getting hand-outs all the time ain't they!'

Mitchell seemed to see that his father's relationship to drink was a two-sided phenomenon. Without a doubt, like the rest of the family, he could see it was to become incredibly damaging: 'His breakdown was probably mostly due to him drinking too much. The business not going well didn't help of course. Down Gravesend you couldn't drive in the market and drive out again, the whole town centre was pedestrianised and you had to park miles away. The big supermarkets started to open up and everyone started using them. His business was going downhill. He should have sold up but everyone thinks it's going to get better don't they. You always think, "Give it a bit longer and it will be alright", 'cos he had been doing really well. But it didn't get better. It kept going the other way. Me mum grafted big time. She was the nuts and bolts of the fruit and veg' business. He used to do the buying and me mum done all the graft. I'm not saying he didn't graft, he had to get up early and he had all the pressure of doing the buying, and if you buy too dear the public ain't gonna buy it. Then he either went home or had a couple of pints with his mates. I suppose he'd had a few quid in his pocket for quite a long time and he'd worked hard and was still working as hard –

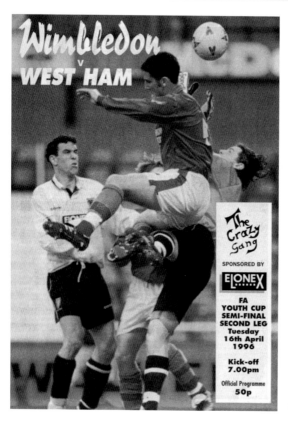

Goodnight Wombles!

it hit him. I suppose all the pressure and stress got too much. Working forty, fifty, sixty hours a week and getting nothing at the end of it.'

West Ham made the FA Youth Cup semi-finals in 1996. Leading the South-eastern Counties League following a 19-match winning run from 25 November 1995 to 30 March 1996, the young Irons had beaten hot favourites Aston Villa 3-0, Woking, QPR, at that time coached by former Hammers skipper and manager Billy Bonds, and Oldham. At the start of April, Wimbledon stood between them and the Hammers sixth FA Youth Cup final. Only Manchester United had a better record. A tremendous crowd of 6,100 had turned up at the Boleyn Ground to witness the battle between the London rivals. The Irons dominated the first half, but were unable to break through, passing up a number of clear chances. As the second forty-five minutes got underway the visitors seemed to gain in confidence and scored on the fifty-minute mark. Wimbledon were having their best spell of the game when Lee Boylan equalised for the Hammers just three minutes later. Whilst West Ham kept the pressure on, with Australian youngster Chris Coyne making notable efforts, it was not until five minutes from time that Frank Lampard junior gave his side a slender lead to take to Selhurst Park a week later.

In south London, West Ham were involved in a real battle, sharing 5 goals with the Wimbledon youngsters. However, following Manny Omoyinmi's brace and Boylan

Frank Lampard, the younger. He moved to
Chelsea after his dad and Harry Redknapp fell
out with the West Ham board.

scoring his second of the tie, his fifth of the competition and his 24th goal of the season
(in 37 outings), the cockney boys cleared the way for the two-legged meeting with the
mighty Liverpool.

1996 – West Ham's sixth FA Youth Cup final: Anfield horror
Sky TV and 15,000 supporters turned up at Upton Park only to see the Hammers,
despite the presence of Rio Ferdinand in their ranks, badly defeated 2-0. At Anfield,
Frank Lampard got the Irons off to a dream start, but the Reds were just too much for
the brave youngsters of West Ham and in the end took the trophy 4-1 on aggregate.

Although the Upton Park kids were overwhelmed in the FA Youth Cup final, the lads
took the South-eastern Counties title, keeping Tottenham at bay in the last few matches
of the season – which is always nice!

Redemption at Tesco
When I first began to interview John he looked slim and fit. He explained: 'A friend who
lives nearby, Gary Levie, said, "We've got to do something about you" and I started
working with him on the buildings. I was about six months with him, and it got me
motivated.'

Former Hammers 'keeper Laurie Leslie, John Charles, Joe Kirkup and fifties striker Ken Tucker.

*I ended up in Tesco through Carol. I'd been ill and it got to a stage where I had
to do something. So she's says, 'Come on John, me and you are going to go out
and get a job'. I said, 'Where we going?' and she said, 'I don't know'. So we went
shopping up Tesco and she pointed out the jobs on the vacancies board and
said, 'Look, go and get yourself a job'. So we both got a job. I took mine but she
didn't take hers. She went round the corner to Sainsbury's. You can't live
together and work together.*

Keith recognised that there was more to his mother's action than met the eye. 'Mum
got him to get a job, to meet people and all that, but he shouldn't have been stacking
shelves.'

I remember when I found out what John was doing, shortly after I started inter-
viewing him for this book – how shocked I was that he was working in a supermarket.
It is not that there is something wrong with the work he was doing – it is that John was
not looked after by the likes of West Ham in particular and football in general, the team
and the game he had served with such tenacity and commitment.

For all this, John used his situation as a form of therapy. He explained:

*I began to work nights in Tesco, Carol works in Sainsbury's. I've been five years
without a drink. I remember going to a book launch at West Ham. I was on the
orange juice with Budgie, and over walks Alan Sealey with his orange and he*

said, *'You can tell who the f-f-fucking drinkers are.* [Alan had quite a pronounced stutter]. *Alan had his illness of course, he was never a drinker.*

When I was on me first night at Tesco I was a stranger to everyone, so I walked in and the manager was introducing us to people and we got to this geezer, with his dreadlocks and everything, young black lad, the manager said, 'This is John Charles', so he went, 'John Charles! John Charles! What, the footballer?' I said, 'Yeah, I did play a bit'. He said 'Where I was born, in East Ham, you're a hero amongst all the black kids.' And I thought 'Am I?' It's life.

Shift work in Tesco is hard work. I wished I was still in football. It is a lovely life now, who wouldn't want it?

John's daughter, Lesley, told me that as children, her and her two brothers often looked at their birth certificates and how her and Keith were always so proud by their father's stated profession, 'professional footballer' and how Mitchell was 'gutted' that on his, the same section read 'Greengrocer'. However, this pride was never something that diverted the family from the practicalities of life – no-one was star-struck by the game, the Charleses were never a family with idols. Even John's exit from football was marked with his pragmatic nature. It was proposed that John would move to Orient as part of Ron Greenwood's plan to bring Tommy Taylor and Peter Bennett to Upton Park. The manager at Brisbane Road was Jimmy Bloomfield. Like Greenwood he was a Highbury man by tradition. Also like the West Ham manager, Bloomfield had spent time at Brentford. Ron had brought him to Boleyn Ground after the best days of his playing career were behind him. Bloomfield was one of a school of gentlemen managers, in the mode of Greenwood, Jimmy Armfield, Bertie Mee (another Arsenal maître d' type) Alf Ramsey and later, perhaps the last of that breed, John Lyall, who would be driven by prudence and a kind of protestant ethic of financial process that was rare at that time. As such he would not continence John's demand for £4,000, which was a lot of money at the start of the seventies. As such, Charlo was never to become an 'O' and would forever be a 'one-club-player' – always a Hammer.

'To give the ball away by virtue of a poor pass is bad enough, but to do it from inside your own defence is deplorable.'

(The Strategy of Soccer – Johnny Byrne)

11

Other Times

'Judging the flight of the ball is more important for a goalkeeper than any other member of the team.'

(The Strategy of Soccer – Johnny Byrne)

1999: West Ham's seventh FA Youth Cup final: it rained goals

In 1999 West Ham again got to the final of the FA Youth Cup, this time against Coventry City. The Hammers were drawn away at Highfield in the first leg. 3 goals in eight second-half minutes left Coventry with a mountain to climb in the second leg at Upton Park.

The Irons made good their reputation as the leading youth team in England by overwhelming the Sky Blues with a wonderful display of attacking football in the second forty-five minutes of the match.

The game was played on a soaked pitch following four hours of rain, but the youngsters from the Boleyn Ground overrode the conditions and in the end should have won by an even bigger margin, having missed a first-half penalty. The Oxford referee, Rob Harris, pointed to the spot in the forty-first minute when Coventry defender Mark Burrows slid in late on striker Richard Garcia. However, Bertie Brayley hit a weak shot and Coventry's massive 'keeper, Chris Kirkland, made a simple save.

But the boys in claret and blue did not let this destroy their focus and assumed complete dominance in the second half. It was the midfielder Joe Cole who opened up Coventry for the first goal in the seventieth minute. It was the product of a brilliant combination between Cole and Adam Newton. Cole split Coventry with a pass down the right flank and Newton sprinted forward to coolly lift the ball over Kirkland into the net.

Five minutes later, West Ham got their second goal and although it was delivered with a modicum of luck, it was reward for attacking persistence. A centre from the left went through the crowded goalmouth and deflected into the net off Stevland Angus. Three minutes later a piece of individual genius from Newton again carved Coventry's left flank open and his low cross left Brayley with the relatively simple job of tapping the ball in from close range.

Coventry's best effort came from Gary McSheffrey in the sixty-fourth minute but his left-foot shot was diverted around the post by West Ham goalkeeper Stephen Bywater.

The second leg of the final drew almost 24,000 people to Upton Park, a near-capacity crowd at the time. Such was the interest in the game that the kick-off had to be delayed by fifteen minutes to allow the many thousands queuing outside the ground to get in. The club did not anticipate that level of support on a Friday night. Only three sides of the ground were to be used for the game, but officials had to open the East Stand at the last minute.

The Irons ripped into the Sky Blues from the first whistle. The third minute had just ticked by when Bertie Brayley put the home side further ahead, following a knock-down by Adam Newton. The wing-back and Joe Cole were outstanding for the Hammers as they thrust forward again. It was Newton who scored West Ham's second of the night in the twenty-eighth minute, ending a fine passing movement by cutting in from the right to crash a powerful left-foot drive into the net off the near post.

Then, Rob Harris, who had sent three senior West Ham players off during the match against Leeds United a couple of weeks earlier and had his dressing room trashed by Ian Wright as a consequence, awarded a harsh penalty against Coventry for a foul by Callum Davenport on Garcia. It was the Aussie striker Garcia who got up to drive the ball into the bottom right corner in the thirty-fourth minute, so scoring in every round of the tournament.

The lead was increased after 59 minutes. Carrick's cross from the left was struck 'goalward' by Brayley, only to cannon off Coventry defender, Thomas Cudworth. But the ball came back to Brayley, who was able to slide-poke the ball home for West Ham's fourth and take his tally in the competition to 6 goals.

Carrick's venomous 20-yard volley against the crossbar could have been the goal of the match, but his disappointment did not last for long. Garcia took the ball into the area with just 14 minutes of the game remaining. He squared the ball for Carrick to hit home. The sixth goal was again created by Carrick as he broke through the middle to supply Garcia for his eighth goal of the Cup run as the final seconds of the match died.

Coventry had simply been overwhelmed. Their only real efforts came in the first half when Stephen McPhee chipped the ball over the bar after goalkeeper Stephen Bywater was left stranded, and then Gary McSheffrey drilled a shot wide. The West Ham manager at the time, Harry Redknapp, and most of the first team were in the stand watching their young protégés and as such witnessed a record winning margin for the competition, beating the 6-goal difference achieved in the 1950s by Manchester United.

Although the midfield dynamo Joe Cole had run the game for long periods, Adam Newton, who had put on a magnificent display, was named Man of the Match before captain Izzy Iriekpen lifted the Cup for the third time in the history of the Hammers. This equalled Tottenham Hotspur's record in the competition and only Manchester United and Arsenal had been more successful over the years.

In the world of football the spotlight invariably falls on the game. The individual is, in the public perception, defined by it, sometimes by just one game or by a single incident in a match. But even football players are people, but no matter how much we say this, the fact never really quite sinks in. I watched John Charles from the terraces of the North Bank at West Ham, then the notorious epicentre of the 'Mile End Mob', the primal 'Inter City Firm'. It was the home of the 'Snipers', the roughly eight to thirteen-year-olds who would one day reinforce West Ham's travelling army of the early

Joe Cole with a radical haircut.

seventies. 'Charlo', alongside all the other players, was a kind of deity, or at least a high priest and, even in my mid-forties, it was at first hard not to see him like this. However, for his family he was first of all a husband, a brother, a dad and a grandad.

The Final Match

The first sign of John's final illness seemed sudden. He had had chest problems for a while, but having been a smoker most of his adult life, this was not totally out of the ordinary. But things got worse and he was diagnosed.

However, less than a year after moving to Spain, John and Carol were obliged to return to Britain as it became clear John would need extended medical attention. But this never really got him or Carol down and John kept true to himself and retained all the qualities his family respected and loved. Keith recalled the situation, 'When he got over his first illness Dad and Mum went off to Spain all bright. We heard about Clivey [John's younger brother] first. Clivey was first to get ill. That was kept schtum. It was a big shock. It was about June or July two years ago.'

Mitchell told me: 'When we found out about Clive it shook Dad up. They was out in Spain. I think I was there. I used to go out there a lot. It was when I worked for BT. I used to work a four-day week and used to get sometimes four or five days off on the trot. He told me Clive was ill with cancer. He seemed very quiet about it. He kept a lot of his emotions to himself. But you could see it affected him. They were alike in different ways. They both liked good food. Their ways were very alike. They even looked alike.'

Clive had been suffering from a form of bone cancer. Keith remembered the very difficult first days after his father came home from Spain: 'Me dad came back in October, that's when we took him to hospital. First of all dad thought he had pneumonia. But it was some neighbours out in Spain, Mat and Kev – Mat was a nurse, who said, "Look you better get to hospital now." Then he came straight back. When he came back I met him at the airport. We decided he should go straight to the hospital. We went up King George's, sat up there for four hours and they ain't even seen him. He told me to go home, cos he was pacing and I was pacing. I phoned me sister and she said she'd go up there. So I went when she got there. Hours later, after he'd been through all the tests, she phoned up and said he's got cancer. I jumped straight in the motor and went up there and he was just shocked. I said, "You alright, Dad? You alright?" And what do you say? He was numb and me sister was crying. Then me mum come back from Spain. Everything just seems like a blur from then. After a while, he'd been going through the radiotherapy, and he came out of it and said, "I've done it! I've beat it!" He hadn't. I always found it tough asking if he was alright and of course he wasn't alright. And I just couldn't get out what I wanted to say cos I didn't know what to say anyway. I just didn't have the words. With two brothers getting cancer so close it was a big shock for Rita.'

Mitch then reflected on his dad's response to the news that he too had cancer: 'You could see he was gutted when he found out that he had cancer as well. He always thought he was gonna beat it. Deep down we knew he couldn't. Well, the doctors told us that the operation could kill him or it wouldn't work. So they give him the radio and he got on with everyday things, just pottering around, out in the garden and that. He coped well with that. But he kept it quiet. The doctors and nurses were fantastic, all of them. But the main doctor who diagnosed it spoke really fast in a bit of an accent. It was a bit hard to understand him some of the times and you didn't always want to say, "Can you repeat that again." But I don't think the old man always heard or caught what he was saying at times. I knew he weren't gonna get better although we all hoped he might. I was up King George's hospital with him, he came out of the doctor's room on his own and he's saying, "Thanks doctor. Thanks very much." I said, "How'd yer get on?" He said, "It's all clear. I beat it." And that broke my heart. Absolutely broke my heart. 'Cos I knew he hadn't heard it right. I didn't know what to say to him. I thought, "If he's happy thinking he's beat it I can't tell him any different." I was gutted.'

Charlie Green told me how he found out about John's cancer. 'I phoned him up in Spain and I was winding him up speaking Spanish. [Apart from being a wine buff – he refuses the title of connoisseur – Charlie has mastered three or four languages in the last few years.] Anyway, we got to speaking after a while and he told me, "I'm coming home because I'm not well." Sad.'

It was so sad. John had come through so much. It is hard for anyone to understand the fear that caused his breakdown. He told me that once he had walked home from the psychiatric hospital where he was being treated and had hidden in his bedroom.

From the time that he first began to feel an overpowering fear, because of his business failing and finding himself 'alone, wondering where all me mates had gone', he had kept a pickaxe handle under his bed. When the ambulance came to take him back to the hospital he was clutching this, 'I was just so frightened. The ambulance drivers soon ran downstairs when they see me with that.' John shook his head and smiled, 'The only way they could get it off me was by getting a mate to tell me he wanted it to use it as an extension for his paint roller. I gave it to him as I felt he was probably nuttier than me!'

Charlo laughed, and although I knew it was such an awful thing for him, his amusement caused me to laugh with him. I was struck by his courage and felt a strong admiration for him at that moment. I thought 'here is one tough man.' And he was strong. He had needed to be. It may be true that he did not experience much racism at school, but this was partly due to him being able to handle himself. He once recalled: 'There was people, at first, who needed sorting out, but I soon put a stop to them.' The same might be said of his experience in football, although he did have his teammates as allies. At a reserve match at Portman Road, a member of the crowd was stupid enough to give voice to his racist feelings. However the bigot was soon silenced when John's defensive partner that day, John Bond, moved from the field of play into the stand to 'dissuade' the culprit from expressing his malevolence any further.

'Knowledge in football – as in all things – is a wonderful thing – and you just can't have too much of it.'

(The Strategy of Soccer – Johnny Byrne)

12

That's What They Called Me

'Think before you act – and always think in the interests of your side. Run, by all means, but run intelligently. You will find that as your knowledge of the game and the moves grow, so you will find yourself thinking more and more in terms of the team's and your colleagues' needs. Move around. Don't be frightened.'

(The Strategy of Soccer – Johnny Byrne)

Although John Charles had finished playing for West Ham more than thirty years before he died, right up to his final days there were many in the East End of London who remembered and recognised him. Although he didn't have the profile of Bobby Moore or Geoff Hurst, or the on-field panache of the likes of Martin Peters or Budgie Byrne, it was these very considerations that endeared him to many. Probably more than anything we love the brave, the fighters and those we can call 'one of our own'. If they are a cheeky, 'chirpy', lovable rascal, all the better. John's character, humour, courage and style made him one of the Hammers' all-time favourites.

For example, Mitchell told me: 'I started this job, first day, 11 September two years ago. Walked into the office, didn't know anyone, bloke called Steve showed me around. He asked me if I liked football. "What's yer team?", I said. "West Ham"; he said. "You'll fit in here. We're all West Ham fans." Steve's about fifty-five so I said "You might know me old man, John Charles" – and he did: it really broke the ice.'

Mitch has used the bridge of football and his dad's involvement to good effect ever since: 'I taught English in Hong Kong, only for a matter of days – it was awful, it was shocking. I needed a job. I didn't know what to do. As you can tell [Mitch laughed] me English ain't fantastic. First of all I was sitting in a class with about twenty people. I had a chat with them but I really didn't know what to say after five minutes or so. I had 'em all going "West Ham United", clapping their hands.'

Fame and family

John's celebrity status touched his children in different ways. For Keith it was something he never registered. 'That's what he did! He'd stopped by the time I was about four years old and when I went to school he was a greengrocer. Teachers at school, like Ken Aston, he was a World Cup referee; he was the headmaster at Newbury Park [Keith attended Newbury Park Primary School then went to Valentines, which later became Ilford High. His brother and sister were also pupils at the same schools]. He knew me dad and he always told me about football, but when you're young it don't really sink in. We were never in awe of footballers. Don't get me wrong, dad knows the likes of John Cushley [a defensive colleague of John's in the West Ham team of the late sixties] and that was great. He took us up to Celtic and into the trophy room. That was something! But now it's a bit different. If you see Beckham, you make a point of pointing him out, but then Bobby Moore and the others were just Dad's mates. Like Lampard, I'd always see him down the Brit [the Britannia pub in Plaistow] – all the footballers were always down the Brit.'

However, Keith's first memories of his father are associated with the game through which most people have known and remember Charlo: 'The earliest memory of my dad was sitting round the telly that was always on in our house. Me mum was at home with us, meself and me sister, and all the kids round the block were always in our house, we had a colour telly, one of the first in the street. It was one of the first games shown in colour – it was West Ham and Man City I think, me dad was playing. I think West Ham got beat. I don't remember him playing but I remember us all sitting round the telly watching him.'

And it seems that Keith is proud of his dad's achievements in football: 'I saw Pat Jennings a few years ago, me oldest was about one. I was down the dogs, it was me first time. I got two kids, I don't go out now.' Keith laughed in a way I recognised well, like Lesley; he had inherited his dad's wry and ironic sense of humour and the ready expression of the same. All John and Carol's children have his laugh – a joyous, indulgent deep giggle, a celebration of a laugh. Keith went on, 'I got all star struck and thought, "Shall I, shan't I?" I'd had a few beers so I went up, called him Mr Jennings, shook his hand, bloody great hands he's got, I said, "Hope you don't mind, but my dad used to play for West Ham – Johnnie Charles." He said, "Great full-back, good man. The last time I saw him it was at Room at the Top [a former nightclub in Ilford]." It was only in later years, when I left the country, that I realised what Dad had done. When you're going through your teens, what yer dad did, you forget all about it, plus I was working for him. And he'd only tell a story now and then. When I got back I realised I missed the old sod.' He chortled, showing the mixture of happiness and sadness we all experience when remembering one we have lost.

Keith gives no impression of regretting not being able to follow his dad into football. He told me, with a good deal of amusement, 'Dad always said me and Mitch had no potential as footballers and that was it!' He guffawed at the finality of it all. Keith quickly added, almost in way of compensation, 'I couldn't keep up with him drinking either.' He rocked with laughter which quickly infected me.

Lesley explained her feelings about her father's notoriety: 'When he finished playing I was barely two years old. It's only the people who know him who know me. You don't bump into people in the street who say "your dad's John Charles".'

For all this, she was always aware of her father's connection with West Ham and, although the club does not play a significant role in the family's life, John's involvement is a definite source of pride. Carol had told me: 'Our little grandson was born with very bad club feet; he's had a lot of operations and needs callipers. Anyway he's got callipers – he's a staunch West Ham supporter, anyway they had to make them for him and he's up

London Hospital, this pair are claret and blue and he's got West Ham United written right up 'em – when he walks along we say, "Jackie, show us yer legs!" and he goes "Oi Oi".'

Lesley: 'We took the kids over West Ham on Boxing Day [2000], the first time they'd been over there. But the club don't play a big part in our lives. Danny [Lesley's husband, a Spurs supporter] plays, he just generally loves football. The kids think it's great that their Grandad played for West Ham because all their mates – it being Dagenham – are just West Ham ain't they. They say, "Our grandad was the first black player!" [Lesley giggled.] They're as proud as punch really.'

However, Carol had informed me, 'Debbie, Keith's wife, is a gooner; an Arsenal fan!'

Mitchell told me: 'When I was a kid it was great cos all me school mates knew Dad played for West Ham. Then, after a while no-one knew who he was. No-one was interested in players from twenty years ago. When I got into me mid-teens I stopped telling people, mainly because they didn't ask me, but I also felt like it was boasting. Then I was in a café one day, when I was painting, and came across a few blokes from East Ham and me mates told 'em and they really wanted to know. So later on it was the first thing I used to tell people.' Mitch giggled at his change of stance.

There is a lot of love in John's family. This is what strikes those who begin to know them well. John told me, without even a hint of embarrassment,

> *The most important thing in my life used to be drinking, but now it's my kids and grandkids, that's it, and a good wife of course. Me and Carol have five lovely grandchildren. Jessica's the eldest, and there's Sunnie, and Erin who's four – they're Lesley and Danny's, Jack, who's a few weeks younger than Erin, and Louis, who will be two next birthday. Jack and Louis are Keith and Debbie's.*

John's sister, Rita, has also been very important to John and Carol. John added: 'If you speak to my sister never even try to say one little word against me. She'll kill yer! She loves her brothers. She is like a mother.' Through her own and John's laughter Carol said, 'She's wonderful. My best friend since I was sixteen.'

Many times when talking to his family it seemed to me that John has expressed the person he was when he played football, or maybe he partly became the person he was because of his approach to the game. For example, Mitchell said: 'Dad was always laughing and joking. He liked playing jokes on other people. He had loads of tricks. He used to go into a pub some days and he'd stick a beer bottle into the corner of the wall. You'd know he'd been in there when you see it. He wouldn't tell anyone how he done it. He used to come out with lots of monologues and limericks and you wouldn't hear 'em again for years. They used to go on for ten minutes some of 'em. I can't recite any of 'em, and I got no idea where he got 'em from. He could be very secretive. You'd say "How d'you know that?" He'd never tell yer. But at the same time he'd never dodged a question. Always to the point.'

It seems that John was not a great one for talking about his footballing days. I have now spoken to and interviewed well over a hundred ex-West Ham players and have found this to be the case with most. This is unlike other sports people I have worked with, for example, speedway riders. John, according to Mitchell, 'talked about certain times, the sixties and that, but never really about football. He'd tell me where they went and what they got up to. It was just a job to him at the time. He didn't watch football for years, not even listen to it on the radio. He couldn't be bothered I suppose. He watched the odd match from the mid-nineties, when the good coverage started – Sky TV and stuff, he used to talk about certain players, "He wouldn't have stood a chance against me" or "I'd have done this or that", "Back in my day". He used to say that the game is a bit harder now. Some of the tackles and stuff he reckoned he wouldn't have got away with years ago. I always thought it was the other way round. I would have thought it would have been worse in the sixties.'

Maybe the football fan is the rightful or logical custodian of the game's memory. This occurred to me whilst Mitchell was relating the following situation to me: 'I went into the pie and mash shop at Seven Kings, just a few days after me dad's funeral, and saw a picture on the wall, and bloody hell, it was me dad. I started chatting with the bloke who runs it and he says, "Yer dad came here a couple of times and I didn't wanna say 'I know who you are'. What I done I got an old programme, there was a picture of yer dad when the team went out to Munich, he sitting on the bench watching the game. I went up to him and said, 'Excuse me mate do you know who that is?' And yer dad said, 'That's me!'." Then they got chatting. When me sister and mum went back to see the flowers a few days after the funeral there was another bunch added, from the pie and mash shop. I was well chuffed with that.'

Best friends – Rita and Carol stunning East London at Stratford Town Hall.

Charlo *v.* Fulham. Alan Mullery (left) and
Johnny Haynes (right) watch, as does
Ronnie Boyce.

John's view of modern players was interesting. He was able to pick out their strengths, but was also clear about their limitations:

Today's players are a lot fitter than what we was. We used to go in, do a couple of hours and that was it. Play a game, do a few stomach exercises, do a bit of running, bit of sprinting, and that was it. The day was over. The hardest part of training was pre-season. Coming back from the lay off. We didn't take much notice of how many games we'd play. After match day we just pissed off and went down the pub. [He laughed.] When I was out on the pitch I wanted to win. I think crowds were for people like Budgie [Johnny Byrne]. We might be 2 or 3-0 up and then Budgie could turn things on. Skill bits and pieces. That Joe Cole reminds me a little bit of him, but he's not in the same class. He's got a few tricks, like Budgie did, but he ain't got the personality that Budgie had. Budgie liked a drink. He overdid it a bit at times, especially when he was injured.

But if I was playing against David Beckham today I'd do the same as I did to the wingers years ago. Make him come across field because he's good on his right stick, but he can't do anything with his left, so make him go on his left stick! Then he'd go half way across the field, then he'd go up in the air. There's no-one to match Martin Peters – Gerrard is similar, but nowhere near Peters. I tell any young player not to be flash. You can't be flash. They get too big-headed and they think they're it. Di Canio, he gets the ball, loses it, sits down on the floor! He wants a kick up the arse! I get annoyed at things like that. If he was playing in my team I'd kill him! I chinned a few when I was at Upton Park. I chinned Cushley. I chinned Stag [Brian Dear]. That's two. Spark out they went. 'Johnnie the One' ain't I.

John heads the ball away against Coventry. In the 1969 League Cup replay against the same club, Charlo was blatantly shoved from behind by Ernie Hunt for the first of three goals in an explosive last two minutes of the opening half – two for the Sky Blues and one for the Hammers. West Ham finished up 3-2 winners.

John chuckled. Making the most precious facet of his personal identity clear he said:

> *They forgot I come from Canning Town.* [He laughed again.] *'Look at Billy Bonds. Can you see anyone getting flash with him? I like the lad Carrick. I don't think Cole and young Lampard* [this was before Joe and Frank junior moved to West London] *would make it anywhere else other than West Ham. Ken Brown was a good player, he would have stopped both of 'em in their tracks. Ernie Gregory says, 'If they're footballers today, Crippen is innocent!'* He giggled.

John continued his critique:

> *I don't think Harry* [Redknapp, at that time the manager of West Ham] *knows anything about football does he? He's just an ordinary man. I've never really seen Harry go out there and train. I think he was right to sell Rio Ferdinand. I don't think he was as good as they make him out to be.* Our conversation wandered to possible successors to Redknapp. We agreed that the then Charlton manager and former West Ham midfielder, Alan Curbishley, was a top candidate. John recalled: *They used to call his brother 'Blower'; he used to smoke 150 Capstans a day. He died a while back. He used to draw them right down.'*

John mimed 'Blower's' smoking action and remarked, 'Lovely fag.'

Happy anniversary!

John's family arranged for a surprise wedding anniversary party for Carol and John in April 2001. They were both amazed by the event. 'They've done me up like a kipper' was John's response at the time. Friends and family turned up in numbers as well as many of his former colleagues from his West Ham days, including Martin Peters, Ronnie Boyce, Eddie Bovington, Peter Grotier, Mick Beesley, Dennis Burnett, John Cushley, Trevor Hartley, Brian Dear, Alan Dickie, John Dryden and Derek Woodley, who passed away later that year. By then John was receiving treatment for cancer but was looking well. I was honoured to be invited. It was a nostalgic and moving evening. Lesley told me, 'I was arranging the do around my uncle coming over. The timing was so great, because Clive's only over every so often. Mum and Dad were unsure if they were coming and I spoke to my Uncle Clive – he said if he was coming over it would be at that time, so I just went with that time.'

Carol related that, 'At first they told me they were taking us for a meal. Then they said we're not going to a meal, we're going to a family do. John handled it really well.' John added, 'When I see me two grand-daughters coming up I thought "I got 'em. I got 'em now." I turned round and see a few of me mates from school! Lesley did well! Not half. People come from all over the place and it wasn't a free bar. Brilliant!'

Rita (John's sister) and Carol (John's wife) babysitting.

Above: Brian Dear, Carol Charles and Martin Peters are at John and Carol's anniversary celebration.

Below: John is with his grand-daughter, Jessica.

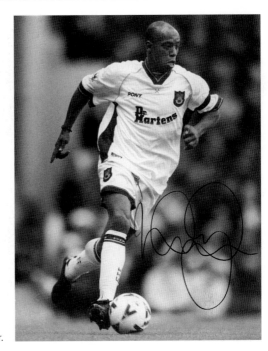

Ian Wright – temporary Hammer.

I missed the first part of the festivities, coming straight from the airport following a working trip to the Far East. I went up to John and told him why I was late. His response was typical, 'Ain't they got fast planes out there then?'

I asked John how he was going to fill in his time now he was not working. He replied, 'I ain't got a lot to do outside, the only thing I'll be doing is a bit of gardening. I like me gardening. I'm always about, sort of thing, less I pop somewhere. You can help me with the garden. I'll scratch your back so you can scratch mine.' He smiled. He told me that he had visited the West Ham training ground some time ago and introduced himself to Ian Wright as 'Johnnie the One'. I did not understand. 'That's what they called me', he said. Then he took me out to his kitchen and showed me a West Ham team photograph on the wall. John was standing in the back row. 'I'm "Johnnie the One",' he laughed, pointing at the print. 'You know something about all those players, who's alcoholic?' He laughed as he asked the question. I looked for a few seconds and clicked. His was 'the one' black face. John chuckled.

'There is tremendous satisfaction for the player who has really mastered the art of dribbling with the ball...Dribbling can be mastered by a number of methods, but it must always be used in the interests of the team.'

(*The Strategy of Soccer* – Johnny Byrne)

133

13

We will Build our Own Society

The great flood of tears that we've cried
For our brothers and sisters who've died
Over four hundred years
Has washed away our fears
And strengthened our pride
Now we turn back the tide

We will no longer hear your command
We will seize the control from your hand
We will fan the flame
Of our anger and pain
And you'll feel the shame
For what you do in God's name

We will fight for the right to be free
We will build our own society
And we will sing, we will sing
We will sing our own song

When the ancient drum rhythms ring
The voice of our forefathers sings
Forward Africa run
Our day of freedom has come
For me and for you
Amandla Awethu

We will fight for the right to be free
We will build our own society
And we will sing, we will sing
We will sing our own song

These, UB40's words, greeted those of us who were ushered into the little chapel at East
London Crematorium on 30 August 2002 for the funeral service of John William Charles.

I had arrived at the Cemetery at around 2.45 p.m. The service before John's cremation was due to take place at 3.30 p.m. There were already about 100 people around the front gates when I got to the entrance of the Cemetery in Hermit Road E16, not too far from where John, the player and I, the fan, had been born, about a decade apart. I watched the anonymous, the infamous, the forgotten and the famous arrive. I stood outside the chapel which stands at the end of the avenue that starts at the cemetery's old iron gates. I saw John's cortège melt through the throng of bodies – the black horses pulling the hearse were led by a group of small figures, John's grandchildren, wearing the 2002/03 away shirts of West Ham United. As the procession halted near where I was waiting, I saw that each of the children's shirts had the name 'Charles' emblazoned on the back, just above the number three, the field placing that, at the Boleyn Ground, will always be associated with Charlo.

I took a standing place at the back of the Chapel. It was crowded but quiet. The crowd outside had trebled in the hour. *Sing Our Own Song* was playing softly. The words seemed right for a man who had made his own life and who had broken so many barriers associated with colour; 'We will build our own society, we'll fight for the right to be free…forward Africa run.' As I listened I recalled a series of limited-edition prints UB40 had commissioned at the start of their *Labour of Love* project. One was called 'Whoever put the word 'race' after human was a fool.' John had, by his life and outlook, certainly confirmed that proposition. Later I was to ask his son Keith about this choice. He told me 'Mum and Dad liked all the fifties and sixties stuff, but he liked 'Sing Our Own Song'. The bit he liked of that was the diddle-lid-did-do; they played it at their anniversary party. He'd sing it with the kids and they'd see him and sing it.'

Again, John had shown himself as a man who could harness love to a cause and in doing so say so much more. The simple and the complex yet again came together in John. He had a way of getting to you without you knowing it. Maybe Bobby Moore learnt that sort of thing from Charlo. I could almost hear John say 'See! Right?' – a speech in two words.

John's coffin was brought in, borne by his family. As he passed me I kissed my hand and touched the cool wood of the coffin bedecked in flowers. It was not so much goodbye as 'See yer later.'

During the service we also heard *Time of My Life*. Keith told me: 'He like that *Time of my Life,* because that's what he felt he'd had.'

It was clear that although it was a sad day, John's family wanted us, as much as anything else, to celebrate his life. Brian Dear maybe came close to saying what everyone felt when, back at John and Carol's home after the funeral he commented: 'John's death was very sad news, but in a way it was a release. He'd had a long and painful fight against cancer. The last year-and-a-half had been so difficult for him, but he battled bravely with the disease and I'm glad he doesn't have to suffer any longer. John was just a lovely man who, through and through, was West Ham.'

As we filed out of the chapel we listened to *Always Look on the Bright Side of Life*. That was so typically John. I waited until nearly everyone had exited before I, too, left the cool shadows of the little stone building. As I went out into the sun that had broken through the shroud of clouds that had covered East London for most of the day, Eric

Up the 'Ammers.

Idle sang the last few lines of 'Bright Side' and I caught…'Cheer Up Brian!' And again, I heard John's voice and felt his spirit. So I did as any eight-year-old Hammer would do when instructed by their FA Youth Cup winning skipper – what I was told.

Outside, everyone – John's family, his friends from his earliest days in football, Reg Leseurf, and players from across the generations of living claret-and-blue history including Brian Dear, John Cushley, Martin Peters, Trevor Brooking, Ronnie Boyce, Frank Lampard, Harry Redknapp, Colin Mackleworth, Ernie Gregory, Lawrie Leslie, Alan Dickie, John Cushley, Mick McGiven, Rob Jenkins – former physio, current coaches, Roger Cross – a striker from the Charlo era, and Tony Carr, gathered round as John's grandchildren released four white doves.

Once high in the air, the first three birds turned in unison and flew roughly in a north-easterly direction, satisfyingly towards West Ham's Upton Park home. The last dove to be released swung high into the sky, away from the others and towards the Thames. At altitude it hung in the blue for a long second, seemingly looking down on the East End and the little clutch of cockneys, young and old, smiling into the azure, surrounded by flowers and trees: the 'we' who had built and were building our own society, in our way, in our time – not black or white, but a satisfying mixture, a harmony of hues, the 'we' who will always look on the bright side of life, the 'we' who will have the time of our lives. Supporting West Ham might be part of that – dealing with joy and disappointment, sorrow and euphoria, the anger, the pain, the exhilaration, the fun…life, not for us the 'Field of Dreams', the relationship premised and sustained only on success – reality is preferred. Living with imperfection helps us develop the humane qualities of support; loyalty, protectiveness, sympathy, empathy and at best, love. It has put me and many others in touch, in a very real way, with John Charles and his family. That is something just not possible now. It is something that those who worship Beckham and Owen will never know, unless they fail, but then who will want to know them?

Finally, the feathery white maverick darted after its companions, catching up fast from the back ('forward Africa run'). 'That's Charlo that one', someone said to the accompaniment of a ripple of laughter. And do you know, I think they were right – after all, he was 'Johnnie the One'.

'Never allow the ball to run too far ahead…As confidence comes so you can move at a slightly increased pace. Do not worry if progress seems slow. The important thing here is to get the 'feel' of the ball.'

(The Strategy of Soccer – Johnny Byrne)

14

Conclusion

'Keep hard at the practising, don't get downhearted at the progress made and never forget that you can always improve your dribbling.'

(*The Strategy of Soccer* – Johnny Byrne)

John Charles was a black man, playing professional football for West Ham United, the East End club, in the sixties. From his own testimony he had no problems with racism from his home fans and dismissed the suggestion that there might be as 'rubbish'. This is not the kind of thing headlines are made of, especially when one considers that accusations about the racism of West Ham fans have, over the years, helped fill newspaper columns and books, for example see John Barnes (1999 p.93), who contradictorily nearly joined his friend Harry Redknapp at Upton Park in 1997 (ibid p.257) but the money was not good enough, and see also Les Ferdinand (1997 p.117) who confusingly actually became a Hammer in 2003. Barnes has since made a name for himself in combating racism in football.

As such, John Charles was a mould-breaker, not just in terms of his being the first black player to play for West Ham and make a mark in top-flight football in London, but also because he steadfastly refused to fit into the predominant stereotype of 'the black footballer'. He, almost belligerently, lived his life on his own terms and formed his own values based on his impressions and experience. He was always a person first. He did not bow to the whims of the tsars of the media, nor the national football establishment and the hierarchy of hangers-on it has produced. He stood up to the dictatorship of management at West Ham and was never in awe of the so-called 'stars' of the game. He never even came close to allowing himself to be identified only or mainly by his colour. This is why I have chosen in this book, first and foremost, to present the life of the man who was John Charles.

For all the toughness he had been obliged to hone, he was a kind and essentially gentle man. He once told me of a reserve match with Chelsea. A number of the players at the time were having problems with alcohol and were, according to John, 'sweating booze.' There had been a scramble to clear the goal line, players were falling and diving everywhere.' He chucked as he described the scene, but he became serious as he told me, 'I just struck out, in hope of catching the ball, or one of their attackers. Anyway, I've kicked me brother Clive! Of all the people I could have caught, I got him. Christ! I thought I'd crippled him. Thankfully he was alright, but I guess the drink was partly to

Jack takes John and Carol for a walk in
Barkingside in the late 1990s.

blame for that.' He nodded thoughtfully and then gave his usual little laugh, but this
time it seemed to be in response to a feeling of non-belief and relief. But this also shows
John to have been a man who would act. He had little time for theory:

> *I never really knew what Greenwood was on about in his team talks, and he
> told me a few times to go steady on the physical stuff. He wanted you to stop
> people but didn't like what you had to do to do that. Me and Mooro would have
> a laugh about that at times, but it stopped people like John Cushley from
> playing, so he never got the respect he deserved.*

Again, John was thinking of another person, but it is also likely that, for the same
reasons, we never got to see John's full potential. He was never allowed to develop in
the same way other gladiators of the game were, for instance Nobby Stiles, Norman
Hunter, Ron Harris and Tommy Smith –all of whom John had encountered and bettered
as a youth player.

John and his wife Carol did not hoard a record of John's career. In fact there is very
little material connected with John's footballing days. Carol told me: 'When John's
mum moved from her house down at West Ham, they cleared the house out and all the
photos of John and his medals all just went. So we had nothing. As time went on I
started phoning up the papers, getting photos off of people, programmes, photo-
copies. I asked for, begged for them. I had a lovely stash of photos and I was working
up the Chequers fruit stall over the road and Tony, the governor there, said he'd like a
look. I took 'em in and someone burnt his stall down and all me photos are in there.'

But she started collecting them again and many of the illustrations in this book have
been gathered by her efforts. I would like to thank her so very much for all her help

Jack is with Lesley, Carol, Sunnie, Jessica and John in the late 1990s.

and kindness and all John's family and friends that have made this book become a reality over the best part of a decade. I would especially like to express my appreciation to Rita, Lesley, Keith, Mitch, Brian Dear, Terry Connelly, Charlie Green and Reg Leseurf. Most of all – thank you John! At one point in our conversations, John had a philosophical moment. Seemingly thinking out loud he remarked: 'Maybe some young local kids can get motivated by this, instead of sitting in watching the telly.' Well, perhaps this will happen or has happened. What is for sure, John, is that you made a difference. The world cannot ask for more.

John's brother Clive died in 2003. Like John and their mother, Jessie, he passsed away in the month of August. The list of '60s Hammers who have died prematurely grows: Clive joins John, Derek Woodley, Dave Bickles, Harry Cripps, Johnny Byrne, Alan Sealey, Les Sealey, Ron Brett, Noel Dwyer and Bobby Moore. It seems heaven may be Claret and Blue....

'I've always been a firm believer in players kicking well with both feet...The question of fitness can, in certain cases, be nothing more than mind over matter. From my earliest days I've always tried to make the ball do the work. Why run with it when a pass can be made and a return pass taken? Make your mind up in good time – and don't change it.'

(The Strategy of Soccer – Johnny Byrne)

15

Elegy for a Hammer

'Constructive use of kicks can leave a rival defence in the realms of uncertainty. Always study the goalkeeper.'

(The Strategy of Soccer – Johnny Byrne)

A friend from the dawn of the claret-and-blue days

This is the second part of the address given by Brian Dear at the funeral service of John Charles on 30 August 2002. Like the first part, it is included by the request of John's wife Carol and with the permission of Brian Dear.

John the man

John had a full life after leaving football. He joined forces with his father and brother-in-law to work the markets in a thriving fruit business, ably assisted, of course, by Carol. John was from a large family – their home was in Ronald Avenue, Canning Town. Head of the family was Big Jessie, whom I know from experience kept John's brothers, Len, Bonzo, Clive and sisters, Jessie, Josie, Margaret, Rita plus Carol and Clyde Best under complete control. What a mum!

John finally left the fruit business and had maybe, as most of you know, a couple of years when things could have been better for him and his family, but John overcame this and became an even stronger more determined person. John and Carol went to Spain to start a more relaxed life and all was looking bright for the Charles family. Then I received the telephone call which changed everybody connected with John in every way. How do you take in that a friend of forty years has eighteen months to two years to live because he has inoperable lung cancer? So we are now here to grieve with all his family who have over the last two years given undying support to John and Carol.

Dear Carol, John's wife and soulmate for forty years. For two years Carol has never left John's side, showing such strength and fortitude. There was never a time, day or night, that she was not making sure that John suffered as little as possible. I know there were times when Carol was despairing. What more could she do? But then came the back-up force – John's wonderful kids who he adored. Daughter Lesley, who was by John every minute she could be, Keith and Butch, his sons, who also gave their mother the utmost support. John was so proud of them. What a family!

The most recent love of John's life was his five beautiful grandchildren, Jessica, Erin, Sunnie, Louis and Jack. He loved them so much. Sadly he never had time to enjoy them

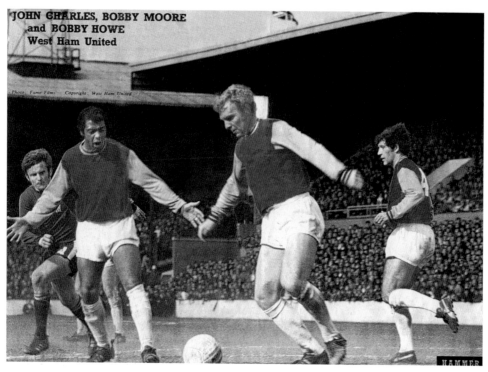

A derby day at Upton Park. John holds off John Hollins, allowing Bobby Moore to set up and attack. Bobby Howe covers.

for longer, but they will always have his love with them. I am sure that Carol, like me, would want to thank everyone who has given support during John's illness: Bozzy, Doll, Frank Mac, Gloria, and Cush and Mary who have travelled down from Scotland on many occasions, neighbours and friends who telephoned or sent messages, finally, a special thanks to all the doctors and staff of King George's Hospital, St Francis Hospice in Havering where John stayed and the MacMillan nurses who looked after John constantly during his last weeks – their care enabled John to rest with the respect and dignity which he would have very much appreciated.

Lastly, you can all be assured that John treated the cancer that took him with the utmost contempt it deserved. As John would have said, 'It turned out nice again'.

God Bless Charlo.

Brian Dear

'What you are aiming to do with the ball must be crystal clear in your mind.'

(*The Strategy of Soccer* – Johnny Byrne)

Heading practice at the
Memorial Ground.

A friend from the terraces

Brian Dear can be seen as the voice of those who knew Charlo in football. His words were reiterated in many messages from those who were involved in the game, destroyers and former foes like Tommy Smith to artists and claret-and-blue allies like Trevor Brooking. There was also a tide of sympathy from fans, too many to reproduce here. However, they are represented by one of their number who was, over the years after his retirement from football, to become very close to John and his family.

During his playing career Charlo liked to bend his elbow with his mates Eddie the Bov, Stag Dear, Budgie Byrne and Mooro at the Retreat in Chigwell, which is now sadly demolished for housing, but, like the great Bobby Moore, he always reported for training the following day. Just as in his playing days, John, when he left the game, was honest and industrious, and he made the most of his abilities in his business when he retired from the football. With his wonderful wife Carol he raised a lovely family that any parents would be proud of, and, despite the problems in his business and with his health in later years, he always retained that inbred cockney humour – a smile was only just around the corner, no matter what.

I am a supporter of West Ham United but John was a friend too. I found writing this tribute very difficult, partly because John was one of the last of the strong, fast, hard but skilful defenders that gave the game the unique balance it had in the sixties, but mostly because he was a special man that carried with him all the best qualities of his East End roots. He was candid, interesting, funny and bright. He was also a caring, loving son,

John Charles shields the ball from the Arsenal skipper and Scottish international Frank McLintock. Northern Ireland international and Arsenal manager-to-be Terry Neill looks on.

parent, grandfather, brother and husband, who always had time for friends, strangers and people in general. I spent half an hour with him just a week before he left us. He was very peaceful – perhaps serene is a better word. When John Charles of Canning Town passed away on 17 August 2002, West Ham United lost another of its favourite sons. I will always be proud to have known him as a player and a friend.

Terry Connelly

And all the rest of us

Of course there were others who had a lot or a little to do with John's footballing fame, who knew this complex, funny and charismatic man. Again, the messages of appreciation and sympathy are too numerous to reiterate in publication, and many would be done an injustice by the attempt. However, with apologies to all those not included below, who I hope will understand have in no way been forgotten, here are a few sentiments collected since John and Carol's last anniversary celebration and his need to leave us, to give the flavour of the vast kaleidoscope of humanity that were touched by John's life across a whole horizon of intimacy.

'From Clarkson School to West Ham United and forever – Love you.'

June and Jimmy Charles

'You're writing a book about a really lovely person. Big hearted guy John.'

Charlie Green

'He was just a laugh John, he was good fun. After he left West Ham he just drank himself silly, drank and smoked. I'll always remember that laugh. His giggle.'

Reg Lerseurf

'John and Carol – I love you. You both treated me with love. So love to you two, to bits, always.'

Clyde Best

'...we will miss recalling the good times we had years ago and a thousand laughs as you recall the numerous stories which seem to get better every time they are told.'

Harry Redknapp, Frank Lampard Snr.

'One thing is certain, nobody battled harder than you to be a player. You were always up for a battle and generally won. What good days they were, we all had to stick together and help each other succeed.'

John Lyall

'A sad day. John played in the first match I ever saw at the Boleyn. I got his autograph as a kid and still remember him taking the mickey out of me for calling him "Mr Charles", to which he replied, "Only the bank manager calls me that!" Rest in Peace, John.'

Gordon Thrower

'A sad day indeed. John used to have a fruit stall on the market outside the Blind Beggar pub [so did Lampard Senior, but what a contrast in men!]. My family had the stall next door. John also had a stall in Deptford market, and Dad looked after it while John went to lunch. Dad was pleased he'd sold a whole box of John's peaches; John wasn't. They were the crappy ones that you were supposed to put in one at a time amongst the good ones! John was a great man, a great player, and a true Hammer. A dignified pioneer in the age when Enoch Powell was advocating sending all black people back "home" [I think to Canning Town in John's case!]. Dad says he was always smiling, laughing and having a joke – a great bloke. I'm gutted. Rest in Peace, John.'

Graham

'May I add my tribute to the sad death of John Charles. As has been said, John was a very nice man, one who became one of the first black men to become a regular in the top division of the football league...a very good young player who gave more than 100 per cent in every game. All I can say is that, being a good honest player and West Ham through and through, he will be remembered by my generation. For the benefit of you younger Hammers, the nearest player I can think of at this time to compare him with would be George Parris, who also gave everything to the club. So to John Charles – always a Hammer – Rest in Peace.'

Brillo

'John – thanks for your style of football, it was a pleasure to watch and gave great enjoyment. May you and Mooro continue with Les Sealey and the other great Irons up there to carry on the tradition with good-style football. Thanks again mate, you enjoy your rest. A fine full-back.'

Baz

'Very sorry to hear of the death of John Charles. He was a true gent who was only too happy to stop for a chat and sign an autograph. A nice bloke, a Hammer through and through. He played with a passion and an honesty that some of the boys in claret and blue sadly lack today. Rest in Peace.'

Hong Kong Hammer

He retired too young and died too soon,
He could tell a good joke and hold a tune.
Chopping down strikers, then up the wing he'd attack,
God must need a laugh and a good full-back.

He was the best of his time; defender of family and goal,
Footballer, husband, Hammer, and a good soul.
Dad, greengrocer, brother, East Ender,
Grandad, comedian and hard man contender.

Truth teller, honest John, no bullshitter he,
A friend to those he knew well and the stranger that was me.
Then and now forever, West Ham's favourite son
The one and only Charlo, 'Johnnie the One'.

Brian Belton

Last words

'I used to go with him to Gravesend, more than I did to Spittlefields, from when I was no more than four or five. He had a Bedford TK lorry. Down on the floor, on the passenger side, there used to be a clear bit of glass that you could see out of. The earliest thing I can remember is being in the lorry with him and sitting on the floor looking out this little window. Now that would probably be seen as dangerous. He sometimes took me sister and he used to get us all singing "London's Burning", one at a time, with Dad starting and then me sister would join in, then there was three of us all singing at different times, "London's burning, London's burning"'.

Mitchell Charles

'It's terrible actually. My earliest memory of my dad is that I remember being where me grandad Ernie had his yard, in Stepney. It had big doors and there was a little green door, there was me and both me brothers. We was with me dad this particular day, it was unusual because we were always with me mum, we were doing bits and pieces and they was loading the lorry up with fruit and veg' and everything. This is so embarrassing!' She smiled again. 'I wanted to go to the toilet! I was only little, about five I suppose. He held me out over the drain hole! He was huffing and puffing and blowing, "Oh my gawd", and that. That's my earliest memory of him. He was a lovely, lovely man.'

Lesley Charles

'He'd come out with a few stories, but you could never ask him about West Ham – he wouldn't answer yer. He had to tell you. How's he's been with yerself – that's strange for me. Most of the people at the funeral the old man had chinned at one time or another. There was the footballers, the greengrocers, the gangsters and the East End crooks. Tom, Dick and Harry. The amount of people he knew and come to pay their respects was amazing really. It's good. The old man liked a joke. Dad'll be remembered as liking a good laugh and a drink.

He was a strange one my dad. When he was dying I know he was scared, but he wouldn't show it or let it get him down. He was "Johnnie the One"'.

Keith Charles

'He was so much like our dad. He was a lovely dad. But you had to behave. If someone walked into the house, an adult, and there was a child sitting on a chair, they'd have to get up. You never said "what" or "hey." It was "yes Mum" or "no Dad". John was a good dad.'

Rita, John's sister

John's younger brother, Clive, who at fifty was still fighting like the East End boy he was against inoperable bone cancer, was able to be at John's bedside just days before his brother passed on. He left John with this message:

'These last few months have been difficult for both of us and our families. It would be so easy to feel sorry for ourselves, to say "why us?", to give in, to stop trying, but that is not our way. We both have so much to live for.

John, I think of you every day. I've never told you this before, but when I was young you were my hero. I love you very much. Keep your chin up. Keep a smile on your face. Your little brother, Clive.'

John died peacefully on 17 August 2002 holding Carol's hand.

'A player should know his role...Once you have a little freedom in relation to space – it is surprising what you can do with it.

(*The Strategy of Soccer* – Johnny Byrne)

Appendix

West Ham's Youth Cup Finals

1957 – lost to Manchester United

Brian Goymer, Joe Kirkup, Albert Howe, Clive Lewis, Roy Walker, John Lyall, Charles Rowlands, John Smith, George Fenn, John Cartwright, Terry McDonald.

First Leg (home) lost 2-3 – Scorers: Cartwright, Fenn

Second Leg (away) lost 0-5 – (2-8 on aggregate)

Joe Kirkup moved from West Ham with his European Cup Winners Cup medal to Chelsea in 1965 and Southampton three years later. He left football having made 382 professional appearances in 1973 and became a successful newsagent.

Albert Howe played for Crystal Palace from 1958 to 1966 and after 192 outings he was transferred to Orient where he made 91 appearances. He moved on to Colchester in 1969. He retired from professional football in the same year.

John Lyall was injured out of the game in 1962. He became a coach at Upton Park, was assistant manager to Ron Greenwood, and then became manager. He later managed Ipswich Town. He now lives on his farm in Suffolk.

John Smith played in 127 games for West Ham, scoring 20 goals. He left for Spurs in 1960 in a swap deal that brought David Dunmore to Upton Park. He was to play for Coventry, Orient, Torquay United, Swindon and Walsall before retiring in 1971. He died in 1988 at the awfully young age of forty-nine, whilst managing a social club in Harlesden, London.

Once described by Ted Fenton as 'The most exciting prospect in the country', **George Fenn** moved to Southern League Bedford Town in 1959.

John Cartwright stayed with the Hammers until 1960, when he moved to Crystal Palace. He was later to coach the Eagles and also become part of the England coaching set-up.

Terry McDonald was transferred to Orient in 1959 and after 152 appearances he moved to Reading where he finished his playing career in 1965, but he carried on in soccer, getting involved in coaching in the USA, and then was back at Brisbane Road.

1959 – lost to Blackburn Rovers

Frank Caskey, Harry Cripps, Jack Burkett, Eddie Bovington, Bobby Moore, Mickey Brooks, Derek Woodley, John Cartwright, Mike Beesley, Andy Smillie, Tony Scott.

First Leg (home) drew 1-1 – Scorer: Smillie

Second Leg (away) lost 0-1 (1-2 on aggregate)

Harry Cripps was transferred to Millwall in 1961 where he played 390 games up to 1974 when he moved to Charlton. He retired in 1975 to manage Barking. Later he became assistant manager to Bobby Moore at Southend United. After leaving Roots Hall, Harry was the boss of Crown and Manor in London for a time and coached East Ham United. I was honoured to coach alongside him at Sinclair House in Redbridge at the time he was working as an insurance broker for Royal London Assurance. Harry, a true Lion of a Hammer, passed away in 1995 at the tragically young age of fifty-four and is mourned everywhere 'The Wall' echoes and is missed at that southerly predator's Den.

Jack Burkett left West Ham, having turned out for the Irons 141 times. He was one of the seven West Ham players to win a European Cup Winners Cup and FA Cup winners medal. He joined Charlton in 1968 but after just 8 games retired from playing in 1969. After coaching all over the world, Jack now works for the Professional Footballers Association.

Eddie Bovington played for West Ham until 1967. He then left football to devote himself to his business interests.

Bobby Moore is the golden Prince of all the Hammers. If you need to be told about Bobby you really do need to do some reading. He was the greatest player to come out of Upton Park and the best captain England ever had…or will have. He died in 1993 at the age of fifty-two, which was a heartbreak for his family and a catastrophe for football.

Derek Woodley joined Southend United in 1962 where he made 160 appearances. In 1967 he moved to Charlton, but returned to Southend in the same year. He made just 7 more appearances before being transferred to Gillingham where he stayed until his retirement from football in 1970, playing 99 times for the Gills. Like so many other Hammers of his era, Derek did not reach sixty years of age. He was well-loved by Shrimpers fans and is remembered fondly in the 'Far East End', on the blousy northern shores of the Thames estuary, where the murky waters of the cockney river merge with the salty tides of the industrial Essex coast.

Like his friend Derek Woodley, **Mike Beesley** joined Southend in 1962. He was to score 34 goals in 79 outings for the Blues before being transferred to Peterborough in 1965. However, again like Woodley, he was soon to return to Roots Hall and play another 119 games in Southend colours. He went on to coach at the club, until the arrival of Peter Taylor, when he devoted himself to his business interests in the area.

Andy Smillie went from West Ham to Crystal Palace and, during the 1961/62 season, played 53 games for the Glaziers, scoring 23 goals. He spent the following season with Scunthorpe, then moved to Southend where he remained until 1968, appearing 164 times for the Shrimpers. From 1968 to 1970 he turned out for Gillingham on 94 occasions. He now owns and runs a café on the seafront at Westcliffe-on-Sea (near Southend).

FA Youth Cup winners of 1963 plus two players from the International Youth Tournament in Augsburg, Germany.

Tony Scott wore the claret and blue of West Ham 83 times as a first-teamer, before moving to Aston Villa in 1965. 50 appearances in the same colours and two years later, Tony was transferred to Torquay United and, together with spells at Bournemouth and Exeter, pulled together a further 199 appearances in League football.

1963 – beat Liverpool

Colin Mackleworth, Dennis Burnett, Bill Kitchener, Trevor Dawkins, John Charles (captain), Bobby Howe, Harry Redknapp, Peter Bennett, Martin Britt, John Sissons, John Dryden.
First Leg (away) lost 1-3 – Scorer: Dryden
Second Leg (home) won 5-2 – Scorers: Britt 4, Dawkins (6-5 on aggregate)

Four years after the 1963 Youth Cup Final, **Colin Mackleworth** moved to Leicester City, providing cover for Peter Shilton. After three years at Filbert Street, Colin went on to play for Southern League Kettering Town. He was to join the police force on retirement from the game and was, for a time, stationed at Bow, often taking duty at Upton Park on match days.

Following 50 appearances in West Ham colours, **Dennis Burnett** moved to Millwall in 1967 and played a massive 257 games for the Lions, before going to Hull in 1973. However, Dennis returned to the Den for a short period in 1975, but went to Brighton later that same year. After a season with the Seagulls, Burnett move to the USA to ply his trade in Saint Louis.

Trevor Dawkins was four years at Upton Park. After the Youth Cup final triumph he was then transferred to Crystal Palace. In 1971 he moved to Brentford.

After 75 appearances with the West Ham first team, **Bobby Howe** was sold to Bournemouth in 1972. He played 100 games for the Cherries up to 1973.

Peter Bennett was transferred to Orient late in 1970. He made 199 appearances for the Os in the next eight years. He became a huge success as a manager and administrator of the game in the USA, after coaching the American Under-18 side. Much of what the USA have achieved in the last decade can be understood as, at least in part, the fruit of Peter's endeavours.

In his playing days, **Harry Redknapp** was an old-fashioned winger and, although he won England Youth honours, alas, the flame-haired lad was not to become a wizard of the flanks. In 175 games for the Hammers the ginger stick man scored just 7 goals. After his playing days at the Boleyn Ground were over, Redknapp was to grace the playing ranks of Bournemouth, Brentford and Seattle Sounders. When he finally hung up his boots, 'H' took up the foil of management and guided the Cherries to glory, winning the Division Three Championship in 1987; and also to misery, sinking with his relegated ship in 1990. However, this was not the end of the silver path of mediocrity for the ruthless Redknapp. After becoming the Brutus to Billy Bonds' Julius Caesar in 1994 (an episode soon forgotten by the fickle patrons of affable 'Arry), the horse-owning, lovable cockney, became the most profligate manager in the entire history of West Ham United. The dug-out Del Boy spent the club's hard-earned income (derived from massively over-priced replica shirts and some of the highest admission charges in the history of British football). But 'Arry brought something more than a smile to the face of supporters (it was more

England Youth Team. From left to right, back row: Charlo, -?-, -?-, -?-, Tommy Smith (Liverpool), Ron 'Chopper' Harris (Chelsea). Front row: -?-, -?-, -?-, -?-, John Sissons.

akin to ironic laughter) when his raggle-taggle hotchpotch added the grandeur of Inter Toto Cup success to West Ham's CV. However, even this was not enough to bestow immortality on 'Redders'. Those who live by the sword die by the same and as such, West Ham's doyen of the turf found himself being made the Chigwell Captain Blye. He was cast adrift from the Bounty of the Boleyn in a cloud of intrigue and recrimination in 2001. At the time of writing, alongside Jim 'Bald Eagle' Smith, Redknapp sits at the foot of the Premiership with a Portsmouth side that looks a bit like West Ham Lite.

Peter Bennett was a Hillingdon lad who signed pro' in the summer of 1963 after his two-year apprenticeship. Making his debut at Upton Park in the spring of 1964 at the Boleyn Ground against Bolton, he was to make 47 appearances for West Ham and managed to grab 3 League goals. An adaptable inside-forward, Peter found it hard to keep a regular spot in the first team but in his six years was an active squad member before joining Orient in a deal that brought Tommy Taylor to Upton Park in 1970.

Martin Britt left Upton Park early in 1966 for Blackburn Rovers, where he played just 8 games before having to quit playing through injury.

John Sissons was to play well over 200 games for West Ham, winning FA and European Cup Winners Cup honours. He was transferred to Sheffield Wednesday in 1970 and turned out for the Hillsborough men 115 times. He then had brief spells with Norwich City and Chelsea before quitting the English game in 1974. He emigrated to South Africa to play for Cape Town, bowing out of the game in 1983 at age of thirty-eight.

1975 – lost to Ipswich Town

David Danson, Chris Smith, Tony Tuddenham (captain), Derek Fraser, Alvin Martin, John Domfe, Malcolm Hill, Alan Curbishley, Terry Sharpe (Terry Hurlock), Geoff Pike, Paul Brush.
First Leg (home) lost 1-3 – Scorer: Sharpe
Second Leg (away) lost 0-2 (1-5 on aggregate)

Tony Tuddenham moved to Cambridge United in 1976 but after a dozen appearances was lost to League football.

Alvin Martin turned out 469 times for West Ham before moving to Orient in 1996 for a brief period. Long-time club captain of the Hammers, he was to win England honours whilst at Upton Park and an FA Cup Winners medal in 1980. He is now a radio presenter.

Alan Curbishley was transferred to Birmingham City in 1979. He was also to play for Aston Villa, Charlton Athletic and Brighton up to 1993. He made 458 League appearances in that time. He is now one of the Premiership's longest-serving managers at Charlton.

Terry Hurlock played for Brentford, Reading, Millwall, Southampton, Glasgow Rangers and Fulham. He made 454 appearances in the English League game.

Geoff Pike turned out for West Ham on nearly 300 occasions, winning FA Cup winners and Second Division Championship medals on the way. In 1987 he moved on, first to Notts County and then to Orient. Geoff finished playing in 1990, but was coaching at Brisbane Road for two years, and is now working for the Professional Footballers Association, helping players work towards coaching qualifications.

After more than 150 outings for the Hammers, **Paul Brush** was transferred to Crystal Palace in 1985. After over two years and a half century of games, Paul moved to Southend. He was to work with former Iron Tommy Taylor at Orient before succeeding the one-time West Ham centre half as manager at Brisbane Road.

1981 – beat Tottenham Hotspur

John Vaughan, Adrian Keith, Everald La Ronde (captain) Wayne Reader, Chris Ampofo, Keith McPherson, Bobby Barnes, Paul Allen, Steve Milton, Glen Burvill, Mark Schiavi. Alan Dickens replaced Reader in the second leg.

First Leg (home) won 2-0 – Scorers: Barnes and Reader

Second Leg (away) lost 0-1 (2-1 on aggregate)

John Vaughan spent time at Charlton, Bristol Rovers, Wrexham, Bristol City, Fulham, Cambridge United, Preston North End, Lincoln City and Colchester United. When he bowed out of the League game he had notched up 349 appearances.

Adrian Keith moved to Colchester United in late 1982. He played just 4 matches for the Us before moving out of League football.

Everald La Ronde was transferred to Bournemouth in 1983 and moved on to Peterborough less than two years later. He was obliged to leave football due to injury, but now heads up security at Canary Warf, just down the road from the Boleyn Ground.

Chris Ampofo joined Aldershot in 1983. However, he had to quit football through injury soon after joining the Shots.

Keith McPherson was transferred to Cambridge United four years after his appearance in the Youth Cup Final. He had spells at Middlesbrough, Coventry, Newport County and Swindon before making a successful transition to non-League football in 1997. He is now involved in coaching and his own business interests.

Bobby Barnes left West Ham late in 1985. He went on to turn out for Scunthorpe, Aldershot, Swindon, Bournemouth, Northampton Town, Peterborough United and Torquay before moving to the South China Sea to play in Hong Kong. He is now successful in the world of financial consultancy.

Paul Allen made over 150 appearances for West Ham before moving to White Hart Lane in 1985 with an FA Cup winners medal. After close to 300 games in Spurs colours, he was to turn out for Southampton, Luton, Stoke City, Swindon Town and Bristol City before concluding his professional playing career with Millwall in 1997.

Steve Milton was involved in non-League football with Whytelefe after leaving West Ham in 1981, but was signed by Fulham in 1989 for whom he made 58 appearances up to the end of the 1990/91 season.

Glen Burvill left professional League soccer in 1990, having played for Aldershot, Reading and Fulham.

Mark Schiavi finished his professional career in League football with Cambridge United, having also played for Bournemouth and Northampton Town.

Plaistow-born **Alan Dickens** played in nearly 200 matches in the cause of the Hammers, before being bought by Chelsea in 1989. In nearly three years and just under 50 games later, he went on loan to West Bromwich Albion, before spending brief spells with Brentford and Colchester where he finished his League career in 1993. He is now a London black cab driver.

1996 – lost to Liverpool

Neil Finn, Jason Moore, Joe Keith, Chris Coyne, Rio Ferdinand, David Partridge, Manny Omoyinmi, Frank Lampard (sub 1st leg – Lee Goodwin), Lee Boylan, Anthony McFarlane, Lee Hodges.

Subs not used: Chris Sains, Justin Bowen, Danny Sweeting

First Leg (home) lost 0-2

Second Leg (away) lost 1-2 – Scorer: Lampard (1-4 on aggregate)

1999 – beat Coventry City

Stephen Bywater, Tyrell Forbes, Ezomo Iriekpen, Stevland Angus, Adam Newton (sub second leg Cooper 68), Michael Carrick, Joe Cole, Michael Ferrante, Sam Taylor, Bertie Brayley, Richard Garcia.

Subs not used: Lee Richards, Francis Birch, Steve Clark, Anwar Uddin

First Leg (away) won 3-0 – Scorers: Cole, Angus, Brayley

Second Leg (home) won 6-0 – Scorers: Brayley 2, Newton, Garcia 2 (1 pen.), Carrick (9-0 on aggregate)

Many of the careers of the young players from the 1996 and 1999 sides that contested the last two FA Youth Cup finals for West Ham are in full flight, for example **Rio Ferdinand**'s and **Frank Lampard**'s. Others, like **Joe Cole**'s and **Michael Carrick**'s, have just started. And a few seem, at the time of writing anyway, to have ended prematurely. As such, this is not the time to review the contribution of these players to the game as a whole.

However, how many of this crop would make an 'All-time West Ham FA Youth Cup final' team? Well, **Stephen Bywater** and **Colin Mackleworth** stand out for the choice of 'keeper. The number two shirt might be an alternative between **Dennis Burkett** and **Joe Kirkup**. At number three, **Jack Burkett** is an obvious choice and **Charlo** might contest the place, although he played at centre half in 1963. **John Lyall** or **Eddie Bovington** at four, five is **Rio Ferdinand** or **Alvin Martin**. Of course, the number six belongs to **Bobby**, **Joe Cole** at seven. **Frank Lampard** or **John Cartwright** at eight? Given his performance, who could begrudge **Martin Brit** his place? At number ten there are the very different options of **John Sissons** or **Geoff Pike**. **Richard Garcia** must be a candidate for the final front spot.

Few would have the exactly same thoughts as detailed above. In the end it may be better to shuffle the pack, but opt for the forward's nightmare of a back row:

Bywater, Kirkup, Charles, Lyall, Martin, Moore, Cole, Carrick, Britt, Pike, Sissons.
Subs: Mackleworth, Burkett, Ferdinand, Lampard, Garcia.

The FA Youth Cup finals

Aggregate scores over two legs

1953	Manchester United 9	Wolverhampton Wanderers 3
1954	Manchester United 5	Wolverhampton Wanderers 4
1955	Manchester United 7	West Bromwich Albion 1
1956	Manchester United 4	Chesterfield 3
1957	Manchester United 8	West Ham United 2
1958	Wolverhampton Wanderers 7	Chelsea 6
1959	Blackburn Rovers 2	West Ham United 1
1960	Chelsea 5	Preston North End 2
1961	Chelsea 5	Everton 3
1962	Newcastle United 2	Wolverhampton Wanderers 1
1963	West Ham United 6	Liverpool 5
1964	Manchester United 5	Swindon Town 2
1965	Everton 3	Arsenal 2
1966	Arsenal 5	Sunderland 3
1967	Sunderland 2	Birmingham City 0
1968	Burnley 3	Coventry City 2
1969	Sunderland 6	West Bromwich Albion 3
1970	Tottenham Hotspur 4	Coventry City 3
1971	Arsenal 2	Cardiff City 0
1972	Aston Villa 5	Liverpool 2
1973	Ipswich Town 4	Bristol City 1
1974	Tottenham Hotspur 2	Huddersfield Town 1
1975	Ipswich Town 5	West Ham United 1
1976	West Bromwich Albion 5	Wolverhampton Wanderers 0
1977	Crystal Palace 1	Everton 0
1978	Crystal Palace 1	Aston Villa (single leg final) 0
1979	Millwall 2	Manchester City 0
1980	Aston Villa 3	Manchester City 2
1981	West Ham United 2	Tottenham Hotspur 1
1982	Watford 7	Manchester United 6
1983	Norwich City 6	Everton (agg. after replay) 5
1984	Everton 4	Stoke City 2
1985	Newcastle United 4	Watford 1
1986	Manchester City 3	Manchester United 1
1987	Coventry City 2	Charlton Athletic 1
1988	Arsenal 6	Doncaster Rovers 1
1989	Watford 2	Manchester City 1
1990	Tottenham Hotspur 3	Middlesbrough 2
1991	Millwall 3	Sheffield Wednesday 0
1992	Manchester United 6	Crystal Palace 3

1993	Leeds United 4	Manchester United 1
1994	Arsenal 5	Millwall 3
1995	Manchester United 2	Tottenham Hotspur 2
	(Man United won on pens)	
1996	Liverpool 4	West Ham United 1
1997	Leeds United 3	Crystal Palace 1
1998	Everton 5	Blackburn Rovers 3
1999	West Ham United 9	Coventry City 0
2000	Arsenal 5	Coventry City 1
2001	Arsenal 6	Blackburn Rovers 3
2002	Aston Villa 4	Everton 2

Based on two points for a final win and one point for a making the final, the most successful sides are as follows. Where points and goal difference are the same the advantage is given for more goals scored. When teams are still equal, position will be dictated by goals against.

Position	Club	Goals for	Goals against	Diff.	Points
1	Manchester United	54	34	+20	14
2	Arsenal	31	14	+17	13
3	West Ham United	22	25	−3	10
4	Everton	20	23	−3	10
5	Tottenham Hotspur	12	10	+2	8
6	Aston Villa	12	7	+5	7
7	Crystal Palace	3	3	0	6
8	Wolverhampton Wanderers	15	27	−12	6
9	Coventry City	8	22	−14	6
10	Sunderland	8	3	+5	5
11	Chelsea	16	12	+4	5
12	Millwall	8	5	+2	5
13	Watford	10	11	−1	5
14	Manchester City	6	8	−2	5
15	Blackburn Rovers	8	12	−4	5
16	Ipswich Town	9	2	+7	4
17	Leeds United	7	2	+5	4
18	Newcastle United	6	2	+4	4
19	Liverpool	11	12	−1	4
20	West Bromwich Albion	9	13	−4	4
21	Norwich City	6	5	+1	2
22	Burnley	3	2	+1	2
23	Chesterfield	3	4	−1	1
24	Middlesbrough	2	3	−1	1
25	Charlton Athletic	1	2	−1	1

Position	Club	Goals for	Goals against	Diff.	Points
25	Huddersfield Town	1	2	−1	1
26	Stoke City	2	4	−2	1
27	Preston North End	2	5	−3	1
27	Swindon Town	2	5	−3	1
28	Birmingham City	0	2	−2	1
28	Cardiff City	0	2	−2	1
29	Bristol City	1	4	−3	1
30	Sheffield Wednesday	0	3	−3	1
31	Doncaster Rovers	1	6	−5	1

The way of the Samurai is found in death.

Meditation on the inevitability of one's own death should be performed daily, everyday.

When one's body and mind are at peace, one should meditate on being ripped apart by arrows, rifles, spears and swords. Being carried away by surging waves, being thrown into the midst of an enormous fire, being struck by lightening, being shaken to death by a great earthquake, falling from a thousand foot cliff, dying of disease…and everyday, without fail, one should consider oneself as dead.

Hagakure, The Book of the Samurai – Yamamoto Tsunetomo

What a Piece of Work was John

I have, for some seasons
But wherefore I know not
Lost all my mirth
This goodly frame
The Boleyn Ground
Seems to me a sterile promontory
This most excellent canopy
Upton Park – look you!
The brave o'erhanging stands
This majestical stadium
Fretted with claret and blue fire
Why it appears no other thing to me
Than a foul and pestilent Highbury
Of Gonners

What a piece of work was John,
How noble as a pro
How infinite in bravery
In attack and crossing
How express and admirable
In his family how like a naughty angel
In defence of the Hammers how like a warrior
The beauty of the field
The paragon of players

Bibliography

Barnes, J. (1999) *John Barnes.* London: Headline Book Publishing

Belton, B. (1997) *Bubbles, Hammers and Dreams.* Derby: Breedon Books

Belton, B. (1998) *The First and Last Englishmen.* Derby: Breedon Books

Belton, B. (1999) *Days of Iron.* Derby: Breedon Books

Bonds, B. (1988) *Bonzo.* London: George Weidenfeld and Nicolson Ltd

Byrne, J. (1966) *The Strategy of Soccer.* London: The Sportsman's Book Club

Cook, C., and Stevenson, J. (1988) *Modern British History.* London: Longman

Fenton, T. (1960) *At Home With The Hammers.* London: Nicolas Kaye

Ferdinand, L. (1997) *Sir Les.* London: Headline Book Publishing

Gambaccini, P., and Rice, T. (1997) *Top 40 Charts.* London: Guinness

Green, G. (1974) *Soccer in the Fifties.* London: Ian Allen

Hartley, L.P. (1953) *The Go Between.* Edinburgh: Hamish Hamilton

Northcutt, N. and Shoesmith, R. (1993) *West Ham United: A Complete Record.* Derby: Breedon Books

Pallot, J. (ed.) (1996) *The Virgin Film Guide.* London: Virgin.

Palmer, A. W. (1978) *Modern History.* Harmondsworth: Penguin

Ruddock, N. (1999) *Hell Razor.* London: Harper Collins

Wenborn, N. (1989) *The 20th Century.* London: Hamlyn

If you are interested in purchasing
other books published by Tempus, or in case you have
difficulty finding any Tempus books in your local bookshop,
you can also place orders directly through our website

www.tempus-publishing.com

or from

BOOKPOST
Freepost, PO Box 29,
Douglas, Isle of Man
IM99 1BQ
Tel 01624 836000
email bookshop@enterprise.net